EVEN MORE
MATHEMATICAL ACTIVITIES

Brian Bolt

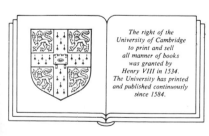
CAMBRIDGE UNIVERSITY PRESS

Cambridge
London   New York   New Rochelle
Melbourne   Sydney

Published by the Press Syndicate of the University of Cambridge
The Pitt Building, Trumpington Street, Cambridge CB2 1RP
32 East 57th Street, New York, NY 10022, USA
10 Stamford Road, Oakleigh, Melbourne 3166, Australia

First published 1987

Printed in Great Britain by Scotprint Ltd

British Library cataloguing in publication data
Bolt, Brian
Even more mathematical activities.
1. Mathematical recreations   2. Puzzles
I. Title
793'.7'4   QA95

ISBN 0 521 33994 4

CK

CONTENTS

Page numbers in *italics* refer to the commentary. An asterisk indicates that a calculator is needed.

Preface

The widespread interest shown by colleagues in both primary and secondary schools to my earlier activities books has encouraged me to put together this third collection of ideas for stimulating children's mathematical thinking.

Problem solving has always been at the heart of mathematics and this has been reinforced by the Cockcroft Report and the paper by the mathematics inspectorate, Mathematics from 5 to 16. Investigations and project work also feature strongly in all the GCSE proposals, so there is a growing awareness by teachers of a need to work in new ways. But to do this they need new resources. This book, together with the earlier books, goes some way towards this in providing a resource of puzzles, investigations, games, projects and applications to challenge the reader and give insights into the fascinating world of mathematics.

Starting with three-dimensional noughts and crosses readers can find how to cut a hole in a piece of note paper for an elephant to step through; learn about the mathematics of stone circles; extend their knowledge of mechanisms; analyse patchwork patterns; learn about many interesting games; make one of Buckminster Fuller's tensegrity structures; become aware of the many problems associated with networks; solve a host of puzzles, and learn many intriguing number facts.

The commentary is an essential part of the book, and in addition to giving solutions often gives further reading and suggests follow up activities. In addition to the contents list there is a detailed index to ease the location of suitable activities.

The HMI paper mentioned above states 'Mathematics must be an experience from which pupils derive pleasure and enjoyment.' This is a statement with which I heartily agree and this book is the outcome of my belief in this ideal. Not everyone will be motivated by all the activities in this book, but there will be few who find nothing to set them off.

Many teachers have contributed to this book: some by making particular suggestions of activities they have found successful, others by their positive response to the earlier books and encouragement to write another. My students deserve a special word of thanks for being the guinea pigs for many of the ideas written up, and once again I would like to thank the CUP editorial team and artists who have taken such an interest in the production of these books. Susan Newell's ability cheerfully to turn my hand-written pages into a neatly typed manuscript deserves special praise, and my wife deserves a medal for tolerating the many weeks I have shut myself in my study to put all my ideas together.

Brian Bolt
School of Education
University of Exeter

1 Three-dimensional noughts and crosses

There are several commercial versions of three-dimensional Os and Xs, such as Fours and Space Lines. The commonest version has four layers of perspex with a 4 × 4 pattern of holes in each layer. Two players take turns to put a coloured peg in a vacant hole. The winner is the first person to obtain a line of four pegs in their colour. There are many possible lines because they can be horizontal, vertical or at an angle. One diagonal line of pegs is shown in the adjoining diagram.

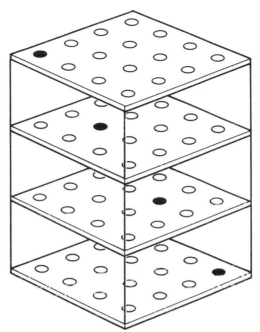

The player who starts usually puts a peg in one of the eight corners. How many lines pass through a corner? Compare this with the number of possible lines through other positions on the grid.

How many different lines of four pegs are possible?

When playing this game you must strike a balance between trying to make a line of pegs yourself and trying to prevent your opponent from making a line. Have you ever wondered what is the smallest number of pegs you would need to put in the grid so that every possible line contained at least one of your pegs. See if you can solve this and decide how they would be placed.

If you don't have a grid try making one using stiff card.

2 Don't be square

Four counters can be put on a 5 × 5 board so that they lie at the vertices of a square in many ways. Two are shown here, but how many are there altogether?

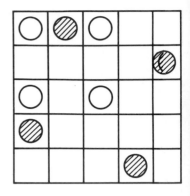

What is the largest number of counters which you can put on the board so that no four counters lie at the vertices of a square?

You could make an interesting game out of this for two or three players. Each player adds a counter to the board in turn and is eliminated if this counter forms a square with three other counters already on the board. The winner is the last person left in.

3 One-upmanship!

Christopher and Elizabeth were working together on a project about square numbers when Christopher announced that he had found something very special about the squares of the eight numbers

$$7, 8, 9, 10, 11, 12, 13, 14.$$

He found that they could be divided into two sets of four whose totals exactly matched:

$$7^2 + 10^2 + 12^2 + 13^2 = 462 = 8^2 + 9^2 + 11^2 + 14^2$$

He sat back, proud of his find, but Elizabeth took a closer look at the numbers. She first wondered whether the fact that 14 was double 7 was important but after further investigation, decided that this was a red herring and tried looking at the squares of 5, 6, 7, 8, 9, 10, 11, 12. She found that these could also be put into two sets with equal totals and began to speculate that it might always be possible with the squares of eight consecutive whole numbers. Is she right?

4   Which rectangles are possible?

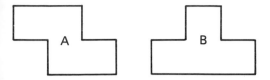

A manufacturer of wooden floor tiles decided to increase the variety of designs by producing tiles in the two new shapes shown here.

Each tile can be thought of as made up from 4 unit squares and they can be fitted together in many ways. Using four tiles of type B it is easy to produce a 4 × 4 square as shown.

Can any smaller square be made using these tiles?

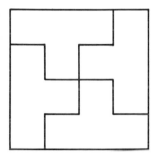

Show how to make rectangles with dimensions 5 × 4, 6 × 4, 7 × 4, 8 × 4 and 9 × 4 which contain both types of tile.

Why is it impossible to make a 5 × 3 or a 6 × 5 rectangle from these tiles? Could you make a rectangle whose area is 210 unit squares with the tiles? Investigate further which rectangles can and cannot be made.

5   Inside and out

Given five hoops with radii 50 cm, 40 cm, 20 cm, 20 cm and 10 cm, show how to overlap them so that the shaded area inside the largest hoop (see the diagram) is equal to the total area of the shaded shapes inside the four smaller hoops.

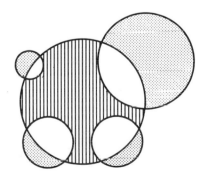

6 A matchstick miscellany

(*a*) Remove only four matches from the 3 × 3 array to leave exactly five identical squares.

What is the smallest number of matches you can remove to leave just two squares?

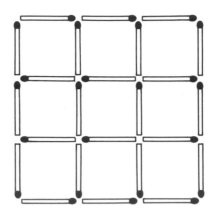

(*b*) Move, not remove, four matches in the Os and Xs grid to form three identical squares.

There are three quite different solutions, can you find them?

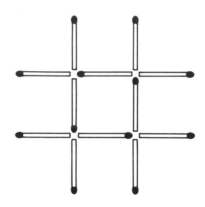

(*c*) Twelve matches are arranged like a hexagonal wheel to form six identical equilateral triangles. Show how to move just four matches to form three equilateral triangles.

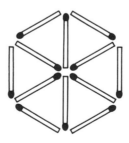

7 Coin contortions

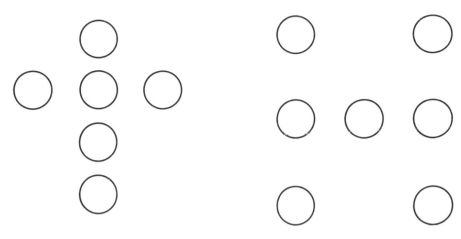

(*a*) Arrange six coins in the form of a cross as shown then move just one coin to form two lines with four coins in each line.

(*b*) Arrange seven coins in the form of an H as shown, then add two coins to form ten lines with three coins in each line.

8 An elephantine hole

A magician challenged his audience to cut a hole in a sheet of newspaper big enough for a fully grown elephant to walk through. No one took him up on it so he quickly demonstrated to them that it was a practical proposition which needed no sticky tape or magic shrinking potion for the elephant.

Can you do better than his audience?

9   Octagonal operations

A regular octagon may easily be constructed using a compass and protractor.

First draw a circle with the compass.

Next divide the circle into eight 45° sectors using the protractor.

Finally join the ends of adjacent radii as shown to form the octagon.

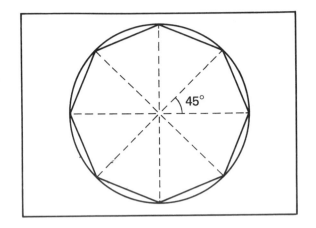

However you can do very well without either compasses or a protractor, for lines at 45° to each other can easily be formed by successively folding a sheet of paper as shown below.

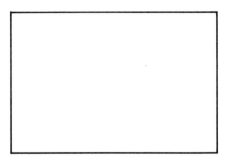
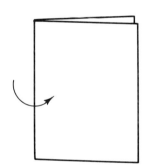
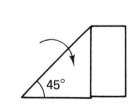

Having produced the fold lines at 45° intervals a ruler can be used to mark off points on these lines which are equidistant from the centre and then the regular octagon can easily be drawn.

Make yourself a regular octagon by folding and cut it out. How many lines of symmetry does it have?

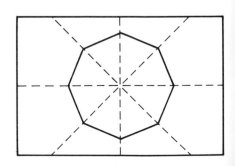

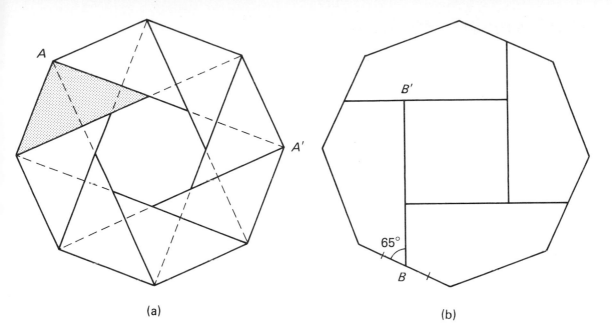

(a)   (b)

Several interesting dissection puzzles have been invented
which are based on a regular octagon. The first, see (a),
divides the octagon into eight triangles like the one shaded,
and a small octagon in the centre.

Given these nine pieces the puzzle is to fit them together to
make up either the octagon as shown or an eight-pointed star.

To make this puzzle first draw a regular octagon on a piece
of card (note if you have already drawn one you can use it as a
template and prick through the vertices onto the card). Next
lightly draw in with a pencil a line like AA' from each vertex
to the third vertex around in a clockwise direction. The
octagon in the centre and the eight triangles around it should
now be clear and can be made to stand out by outlining them
with a ball point pen. Now cut the pieces out and try making
an eight-pointed star.

The second dissection divides a regular octagon into four
pentagons and a square, see (b), which can be rearranged to
form a larger square.

As before, first draw a regular octagon on a piece of card.
Next draw lines like BB' from the mid-point of every other
edge at an angle of 65° to the edge to form the central square
and the four bordering pentagons.

Now cut out the five pieces and try to rearrange them to
form a square.

10 Delving into dissections

Many puzzle books set puzzles based on cutting up one shape in as few pieces as possible which can be rearranged to form another shape. Typical of these is the puzzle which invites you to cut up a Greek cross into four pieces which can be rearranged to form a square, see (a). If the cross is seen as made up of 5 unit squares then the square into which the cross is to be transformed must also have an area equivalent to 5 square units. Two solutions to the puzzle are shown in (b) and (c) but how are they arrived at?

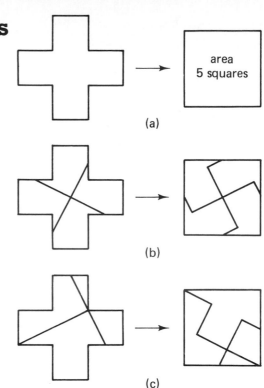

(a)

(b)

(c)

One answer lies in the use of tessellations. In (d) the Greek cross is shown forming a tessellation and then superimposed on it is a tessellation of squares whose area is 5 square units formed by joining the centres of the adjacent crosses.

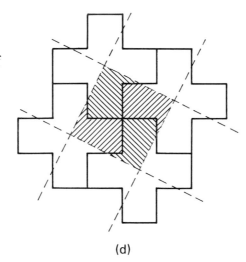

(d)

It is then clear how the four pieces which make up the shaded square come from dissecting the cross. The length of side of the shaded square is √5 units and this is easily seen as the diagonal of a 2 × 1 rectangle by applying Pythagoras' theorem, see (e).

If the tessellation of √5 squares is drawn on tracing paper then it can be moved into different positions over the tessellation of crosses and further solutions such as that in (c) discovered.

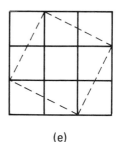

(e)

8

Draw a tessellation of crosses (it helps to start with squared paper) and superimpose on it the tessellation of squares which corresponds to (c).

Use the tessellation method to find ways of dissecting the three shapes shown in (f) into pieces which can be rearranged to form squares.

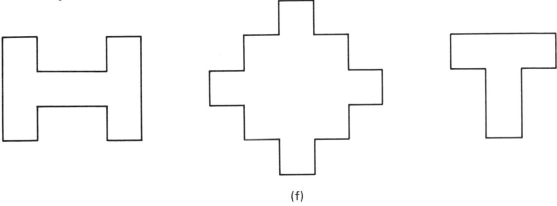

(f)

Another dissection puzzle based on the H shape in (f) is to find a way of cutting it into four identical pieces which can be put together to form two H shapes.

What can you say about the shape of a rectangle if one straight cut can divide it into two pieces which can be put together to form a square?

Given a rectangular piece of card which is 16 cm by 9 cm show that it is possible to divide it into two pieces which fit together to form a square.

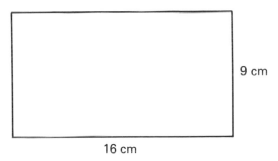

9 cm

16 cm

The dissections so far have all been about transforming shapes into squares, but a notable dissection by Sam Loyd, the famous American puzzlist, starts with a square. Starting with his dissection of a square shown, find ways of rearranging the five pieces to form
    (1) a rectangle,
    (2) a right-angled triangle,
    (3) a parallelogram,
    (4) a Greek cross.

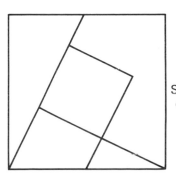

Sam Loyd's dissection

In drawing out this dissection it helps to appreciate that each line inside the square, if extended, would pass through a vertex and the mid-point of one side of the square.

11 The jeweller's chain

A jeweller had an urgent order to make a chain with 25 links
for a local mayor. At the time she had an assistant and five
apprentices so they each set to with a will to make a part of
the chain. The links were large so the jeweller was well
pleased when by 5 o'clock they had made the 25 links. She
then realised how inefficient they had been, for between
them they had seven pieces of chain; two with 2 links, two
with 3 links and one each of 4 links, 5 links and 6 links. To join
the pieces into one chain of 25 links she would need to cut and
rejoin some of the links. She reckoned that to cut and join a
single link would take her 20 minutes so she decided to stay
on and finish the job by herself.

What was the earliest time the jeweller could have gone
home with the 25-link chain complete?

12 Touching coins

(a) The first problem is to place four identical coins in such a way that they are all the same distance from each other. The solution is not a square array, as the diagram shows, for the distance from A to C is more than the distance from A to B. There is more than one solution, but the best has the centres of the coins equidistant from each other.

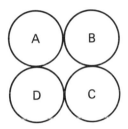

(b) It is easy to place four coins so that they each touch a fifth coin, but how can you place five identical coins so that they each touch all the others?

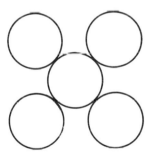

13 Two wrongs make a right

```
  W R O N G
+ W R O N G
  ─────────
  R I G H T
```

In spite of what we are always told two wrongs can make a right if each letter in the adjoining sum is taken to stand for a different digit.
Can you find a solution?

14　Micro millions

The micro millionaire studied his balance sheet at the end of
the year with great interest. The total income from the sale of
the very popular Domomicro model came to £1 000 000 000.
What aroused his interest was not so much the total as that
neither the number of micros sold nor the cost of an
individual micro contained a single zero digit.

How many micros were sold?

15　The economy cut

Emma was always looking for ways to save money. While in
the remnant shop she came across just the material she
wanted to make a table-cloth.

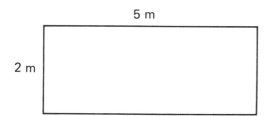

Unfortunately the piece of material was in the form of a
2 m × 5 m rectangle and her table was 3 m square. She bought
it however having decided that the area was more than
enough to cover the table. When she got home however she
decided she had been a fool because she couldn't see how to
cut up the material to make a square. But just as she
despaired she had a brainwave, and with 3 straight cuts, in no
time at all, she had 5 pieces which fitted neatly together in a
symmetric pattern to form a square using all the material.
How did she do it?

16 The area of a parallelogram

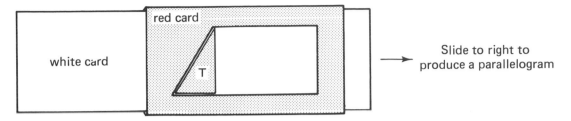

red card

white card

T

Slide to right to
produce a parallelogram

The visual aid shown here is very easy to make and does help
children to appreciate the relation between the area of a
parallelogram and the area of a rectangle.

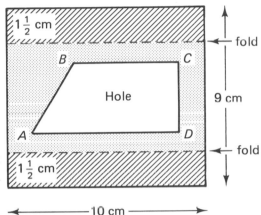

$1\frac{1}{2}$ cm

fold

B

C

Hole

9 cm

A

D

fold

$1\frac{1}{2}$ cm

10 cm

To make this model start with a rectangular piece of
coloured card say 9 cm by 10 cm and cut out a hole
$ABCD$ in the shape of a trapezium which is right angled at
C and D, with BC and AD parallel to the edges of the card.
Fold the card along the lines shown so that the shaded
portions are flat against the back of the unshaded portion.

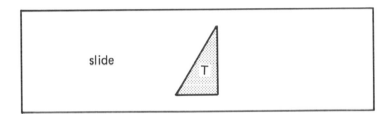

slide

T

Using different coloured card cut out a rectangle
approximately 20 cm by 6 cm. This must just fit inside the
folds of the first piece of card and be able to slide easily.
Push the slide as far as you can to the left. Then stick on it
the triangle T, which is cut from the trapezium removed from
the first piece of card, so that it fits snugly in the hole leaving a
rectangle of the slide showing through. When the slide is
pushed to the right and the triangle is touching CD then a
parallelogram hole appears of the same area as the rectangle.

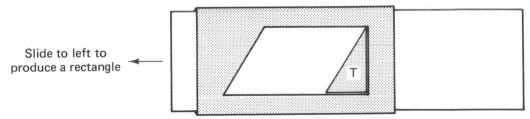

Slide to left to
produce a rectangle

T

13

17   Quadreels

A quadrille is a dance for four
couples. Quadreels is a spatial
game for a couple to play
involving sets of four cotton
reels. It is in fact a
three-dimensional version of
the popular game Connect
Four. Before playing the
game you will need to
construct the playing frame
and collect a number of cotton
reels.

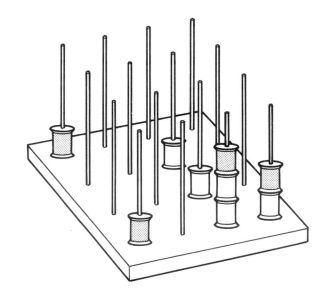

The playing frame consists
of a square base board say
15 cm by 15 cm, in which are
inserted 16 dowel rods in a
4 × 4 square array (see the diagram). The diameter of the
dowel should be about 4 to 5 mm so that a cotton reel can
slide down it easily. The length of a dowel above the base
board should be sufficient for four cotton reels to stand
securely on it.

To play the game you will need up to 64 cotton reels, half of
which should be painted red and half blue, or whatever two
colours you prefer.

Players take turns to add a reel of their colour to the frame,
and the winner is the first person to obtain a line of four of
their reels. The line may be horizontal, vertical, or any
diagonal so there are many possibilities. A player's turn
provides at most 16 possible moves, but deciding which to
take to improve your own chance of a line while trying to
make sure you stop your opponent needs a lot of skill.

18   Folding 60° angles

It is not difficult to fold angles of 180°, 90°, 45° and 22½°
because all that is required is repeated bisection of an angle,
see activity 9. However to obtain an angle of 60° or 30° it is
necessary to trisect an angle. This can be achieved

14

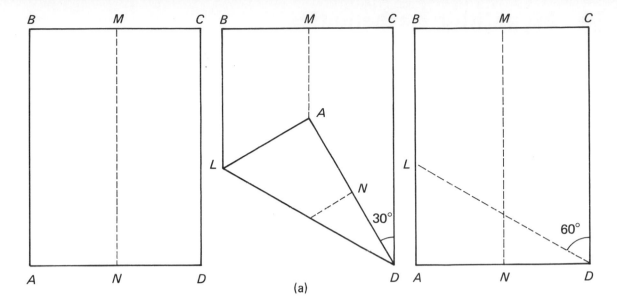

(a)

surprisingly easily. See the diagram (a). Take a rectangular sheet of paper $ABCD$ and produce a fold line MN to bisect it as shown by folding AB onto DC. Now fold the paper so that the fold goes through D and corner A is on the fold line MN. AD is now at 30° to DC and the fold line LD is at 60° to DC.

If the paper is now folded through L parallel to BC, and before unfolding the sheet is folded along LD, then an equilateral triangle is formed, triangle LPD in diagram (c).

By making use of the existing fold lines it is easy to fold or draw in further lines to produce a tessellation of equilateral triangles and make nets for some of the regular solids.

Starting with a square piece of paper fold yourself a regular hexagon.

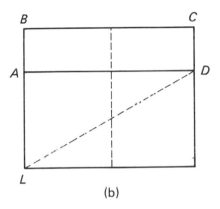

(b)

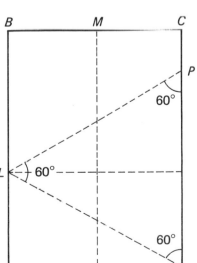

(c)

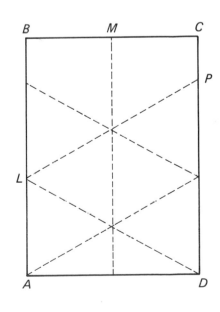

15

19 Megalithic mathematics

Over the years scientists and archaeologists have taken a lot of interest in the many stone circles to be found throughout Western Europe of which Stonehenge is the prime example. The link between the positions of the stones and the position of the sun has had writers describing Stonehenge as an astromomical computer, but here it is the intention to look at the basic shape of the so-called circles. Stonehenge is as near to a circle as makes no difference, but the engineer Professor Thom surveyed hundreds of sites of standing stones and showed that many of the circles were not in fact circles at all but were carefully constructed curves, often based on Pythagorean triangles.

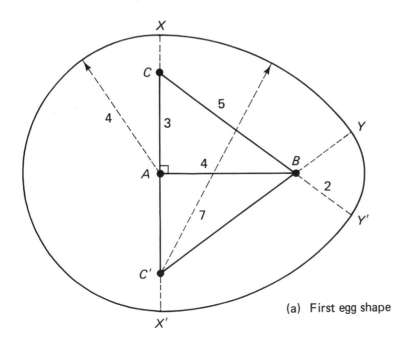

(a) First egg shape

One of the shapes discovered by Thom was like the egg shown in (a). To draw it start by constructing the 3, 4, 5 Pythagorean triangle ABC and its mirror image in AB, triangle ABC'. With centre A draw the semicircle with radius AB (4 units) and diameter XX' on the left of CC'. With centre C' and radius $C'X$ (7 units) draw arc XY, and with centre C and the same radius draw arc $X'Y'$. With centre B and radius BY (2 units) draw arc YY' to complete the egg shape. Examples of this shape are to be found at Cairnpapple Hill in West Lothian, and at Clava in Inverness.

Any right-angled triangle can be used as a starting point and eggs can be constructed by this method to be nearly circular or more pointed. Try drawing some for yourself.

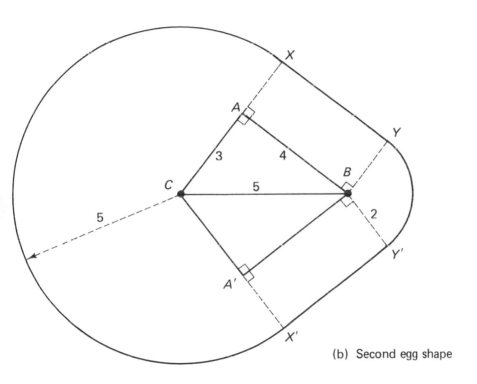

(b) Second egg shape

In Devon and Cornwall a different shape of stone circle is to be found which can still be described as egg-shaped although parts of its perimeter are straight lines, see (b). This shape is again based on two identical right-angled triangles, but this time reflected in their hypotenuse BC. Having drawn the triangles ABC and $A'BC$, first draw the major arc XX' with centre C and radius CB, (5 units). Draw XY parallel to AB and $X'Y'$ parallel to $A'B$, then with centre B and radius BY draw minor arc YY'.

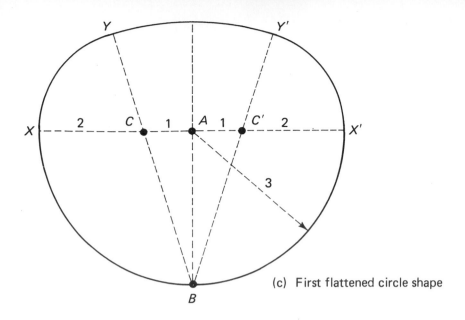

(c) First flattened circle shape

Two further shapes identified by Thom he called flattened circles and the flattened portion approximates closely to an ellipse although again the curve consists of arcs of circles. The first of these is shown in (c) where the portion of the curve below XX' is a semicircle centred on A. Points C and C' are then found on XX' so that AC and AC' are a third of the radius of the semicircle. AB is the line of symmetry of the semicircle and of the whole shape. Arc XY is drawn with centre at C and radius CX (2 units), while arc $X'Y'$ has centre C' and the same radius. The arc YY' is drawn last with centre at B and radius BY. Examples of this type are the stone circle at Merrivale on the edge of Dartmoor, and the 'Long Meg and her daughter' circle in Cumbria.

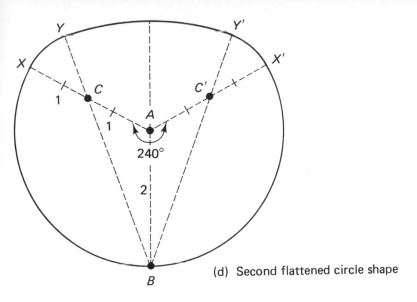

(d) Second flattened circle shape

The second 'flattened circle' shape, see (d), can be
constructed by first drawing two thirds of a circle centred on
A from X through B to X'. AB is the line of symmetry of this
major sector, and points C and C' are halfway along the radii
AX and AX'. Draw arc XY with centre C and radius CX
(1 unit) and arc $X'Y'$ with centre C' and the same radius.
Complete the shape by drawing arc YY' with centre B and
radius BY. A good example of this shape is the Castle Rigg
circle near Keswick and others are to be found in Cumbria
and Scotland.

The interesting property of all these shapes is that even
though they are constructed from circles with different
centres and different radii, where the different arcs meet they
have a common tangent so there is no abrupt change in
direction.

If you live near a stone circle try making an accurate survey
of it to see whether it is one of the shapes discussed.
Investigate the perimeters and the areas inside these
changes.

19

20 Loading the ferry

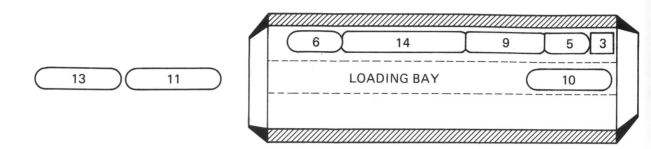

The only way to cross a wide river estuary was to use the ferry. The approach road to the ferry was very narrow so the traffic for the ferry had to queue in single file in the order in which it arrived. The ferry itself had a loading bay 40 metres long which could hold three lanes of traffic.

The person responsible for loading the ferry let the vehicles onto the ferry so that the left-hand lane was filled as far as possible before using the middle lane, and when the next vehicle in the queue was too long for the space left in the middle lane the vehicles were diverted to fill the right hand lane.

This strategy for loading the ferry meant that it was frequently loaded inefficiently, particularly when the queue contained several long lorries. The ferry owner became concerned about this for it was not only bad for public relations but significantly reduced his profits. To overcome the problem a device was installed which measured the length of each vehicle as it joined the ferry queue and fed the information into a computer which worked out the best lane of the ferry's loading bay for each vehicle. As each driver came to the head of the queue and drove up the loading ramp a green light came on over the appropriate lane.

On one occasion the lengths of the vehicles in the ferry queue, taken in order of arrival were

> 3 m, 5 m, 9 m, 14 m, 6 m, 10 m, 11 m,
> 13 m, 7 m, 8 m, 15 m, 11 m, 8 m, 4 m.

Before the computer was installed how many of these vehicles would have been loaded and what percentage of space would have been wasted?

Show that by carefully selecting the lane for each vehicle as it comes to the head of the queue it is possible to load the ferry to full capacity from this particular queue.

21 A symmetric cross-number puzzle

An 8 × 8 cross-number puzzle has most of its black squares missing but they can soon be filled in with the knowledge that the completed puzzle is symmetric about the two dotted lines shown. To complete the puzzle all you need to know is that every number is either prime or the cube of a prime, and that only three different digits appear in the solution.

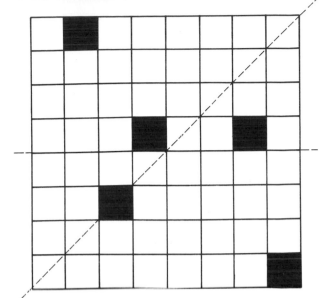

22 A question of place value

```
1 2 3 4 5 6 7 8 9          9 8 7 6 5 4 3 2 1
1 2 3 4 5 6 7 8 0          0 8 7 6 5 4 3 2 1
1 2 3 4 5 6 7 0 0          0 0 7 6 5 4 3 2 1
1 2 3 4 5 6 0 0 0          0 0 0 6 5 4 3 2 1
1 2 3 4 5 0 0 0 0          0 0 0 0 5 4 3 2 1
1 2 3 4 0 0 0 0 0          0 0 0 0 0 4 3 2 1
1 2 3 0 0 0 0 0 0          0 0 0 0 0 0 3 2 1
1 2 0 0 0 0 0 0 0          0 0 0 0 0 0 0 2 1
1 0 0 0 0 0 0 0 0          0 0 0 0 0 0 0 0 1
```

The above addition sums are obtained from each other by reversing the order of digits in each. They have an obvious similarity but which do you think has the larger sum?

23 Another number pattern

Extend and explain the adjoining pattern.

$$1 \times 8 + 1 = 9$$
$$12 \times 8 + 2 = 98$$
$$123 \times 8 + 3 = 987$$
$$1234 \times 8 + 4 = 9876$$
$$12345 \times 8 + 5 = 98765$$

24 The L-game

This is a game for two players devised by Edward de Bono of lateral thinking fame. Like most good games it is easy to learn the rules and play, but through playing the participants can develop skills and strategies which will enable them to outwit less skilful opponents.

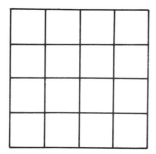 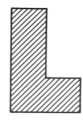 

The board of play consists of sixteen squares in a 4 × 4 array. Each player has an L-shaped piece which exactly covers four squares of the board and in addition there are two neutral pieces equivalent to a single square which can be moved by either player.

The game starts with the L-shapes occupying the central strip and the neutral pieces in the corners — rather like two wellington boots kicking footballs!

A *move* consists of a player moving their L-piece to another position on the board. It must cover four squares, at least one of which must be different from its previous position. The move may be a translation, rotation, reflection or glide reflection or in other words any move which is physically possible as long as the new position does not overlap any other piece.

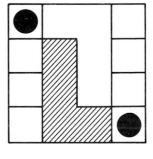

Starting position

After the L-piece has been moved the player may, if so wished, move *one* of the neutral pieces to any unoccupied square on the board.

The object of the game is so to position the pieces that your opponent is unable to move their L-piece. With such a small board it looks deceptively easy.

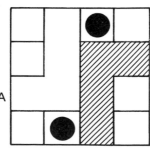

A

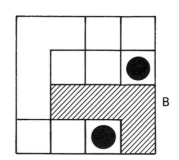

B

Some positions are more restricting than others. From position A white has three possible moves for the L-piece and then the option of leaving the neutral pieces as they are or moving one or other of them to a choice of six positions. Thus, in all, from A white has $3 \times 13 = 39$ possible choices. From position B, however, white has far more scope for there are eight possible moves for the L-piece (can you spot them all) and then thirteen choices for the neutral pieces giving $8 \times 13 = 104$ overall choices.

It is possible to trap an L-shape however and the following diagrams show two winning positions for black.

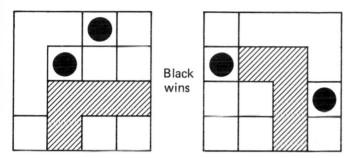

Black wins

Players can spin a coin to decide who starts or just take in turns moving first. No elaborate equipment is required but experience of using the game with children suggests using a board based on squares which are 3 cm by 3 cm. Cut the L-pieces to the same scale out of coloured card. Use a different colour for each L and a third colour for the neutral pieces, although the latter could be counters and really need not be square.

25 One hundred up!

This is a number game for two players involving simple addition. The first player calls a number from 1 to 10. The second player increases this number by any number from 1 to 10.

Players play alternately by always increasing the last number called by any number from 1 to 10. The object is to be the first person to reach 100.

Can you devise a winning strategy?

26 Mancala

Mancala is a very ancient game which is believed to have
originated in Egypt over 3000 years ago and is now played
world-wide but particularly throughout Africa. The playing
surface, see (a), consists of 12 hollows which contain counters
of some kind. It can be found commercially, when the board
looks rather like a bun tin and the counters are plastic balls,
or improvised as in Africa, where the author has vivid
memories of the local champion taking on all-comers at a
market in Lusaka where the playing surface consisted of
hollows scraped in the ground and the counters were small
stones. No doubt the game was played for a wager and it
certainly attracted a crowd of onlookers all giving their
advice to the challenger.

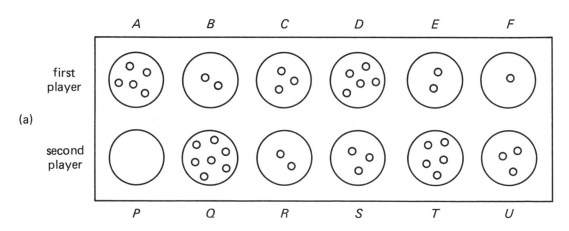

The game has many variants but all depend on counting.

The two players sit one each side of the board and lay claim to the six hollows nearest them. With the above board, for example, one player controls A to F and the other player controls P to U.

At the start 6 counters are put into each hollow.

Each player in turn picks up all the counters from one of their hollows and then counting around the board in a clockwise or anticlockwise direction, dropping one counter successively into each hollow they pass until all counters are gone. If the last counter put into a hollow produces a total of 6 or 4 or 2 there, then they are removed by the player. Further, if the preceding two hollows have totals of 2, 4 or 6 at this stage they may also be removed — but only if the last hollow has already been emptied. When 12 or fewer counters are left then moves must be made clockwise.

For example, suppose it is the turn of the second player with the game in the position shown in (a). That player could pick up the 5 counters in hollow T, and travelling anticlockwise, add 1 counter to each of hollows, U, F, E, D and C. This makes 4 counters in C which are removed and 6 counters in D which can consequently also be removed, as shown in (b).

(b)

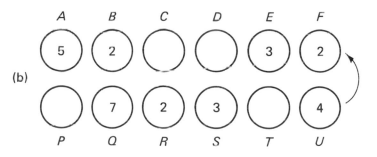

This was a particularly good move for the second player who will not only have gained 10 counters but left the first player with a position where no counters can be won.

The object of the game, of course, is to obtain more counters than your opponent. Counters can be accumulated by a player from any hollow but players can only start counting from hollows on their own side.

A stage will be reached when the number of counters left in the hollow makes it impossible for either player to win any more and at this point the players take stock of their gains.

27 Tsyanshidzi

This is an ancient Chinese game for two players played with two piles of stones not unlike Nim, see *Mathematical Activities*, activity 154. The translation of the name means 'picking stones' and players take turns picking up stones from the piles. Players may (*a*) take as many stones as they please from one pile or alternatively (*b*) take stones from both piles as long as the same number is taken from each. The object of the game is to be the person to pick up the last pebble.

Clearly if you are to win there are certain positions to avoid. There would be no point in leaving your opponent with just one pile of stones or leaving the piles with an equal number in each. But what other positions should be avoided?

Suppose you are faced with the situation where the first pile has one stone and the second pile has two $(1, 2)$.

If you reduce either pile to zero then your opponent wins. The only other possibility you have is to remove one stone from the second pile whereupon there is one stone in each pile so again your opponent wins.

Of course, if you can bring about this position then you can win. Now this position can be readily achieved from positions such as

$(1, n)$ by removing $(n - 2)$ stones from the second pile,

$(2, m)$ by removing $(m - 1)$ stones from the second pile,

$(r, r + 1)$ by removing $(r - 1)$ stones from each pile.

It follows that you don't want to leave such a combination for your opponent or alternatively if he leaves it for you then you can leave a $(2, 1)$ or $(1, 2)$ position and win.

Investigate other situations that can lead to a win.

28 Intersecting lines

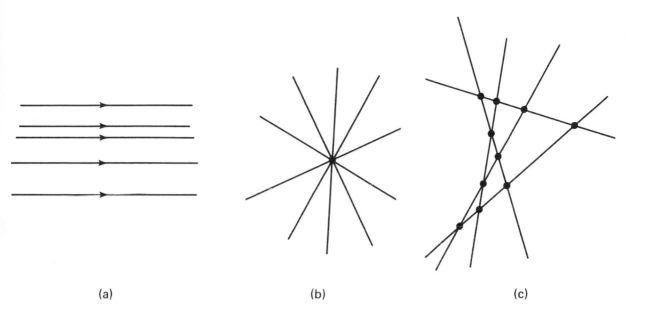

(a)   (b)   (c)

Five straight lines can be drawn in a plane in an infinite number of ways. They could be parallel as in (a) when they do not cross anywhere, or all pass through one point as in (b). The largest number of intersections obtainable is 10 as in (c).

The question arises, can the lines be drawn to obtain only 2 intersections, or 3, or 4, ... or 9?

Some sketches on a piece of paper will soon convince you that 2 intersections or 3 intersections are not possible unless lines are allowed to coincide with each other, but ruling that out there are three quite different solutions for 4 intersections, see (d).

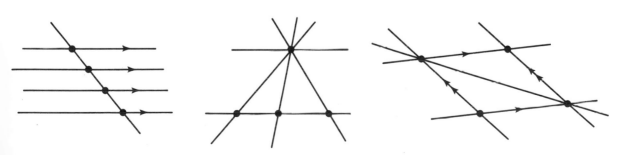

(d) Solutions to 5 lines with 4 intersections

There are solutions to be found for more than 4 intersections, and as with 4 intersections there is often more than one kind of solution. Figure (e) shows some of them. See what others you can find.

(e)

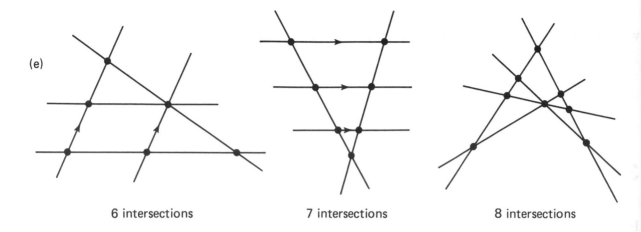

| 6 intersections | 7 intersections | 8 intersections |

Now try similar investigations with 4 lines and 6 lines. In doing these investigations you have probably realised that the numbers of intersections can be reduced in two ways: (1) using multiple intersections; (2) using parallel lines or combinations of the two.

See how quickly you can make use of your experience of this investigation to draw 10 lines so that they make 27 intersections.

29 Make a rectangle

Rachel was told by her teacher to cut out six pentominoes of the shape shown and to investigate how they might be fitted together to form rectangles. It didn't take her long to see that two pieces fitted together to make a 5 × 2 rectangle and that this rectangle could be used as a building block for larger rectangles.

But then she found further solutions hard to come by. She was persistent however and eventually found three ways of making a 5 × 4 rectangle and six ways of making a 6 × 5 rectangle.

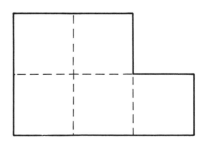

Try as she could however she couldn't make a square.
How well can you do?

30 As easy as abc!

Find numbers a, b and c such that

$$a^b \times c^a = abca$$

where $abca$ stands for a 4-digit number.

31 The dishonest gold exporter

Because gold is such a precious metal an exporter tried to make money by melting down the genuine gold ingots and recasting them in moulds which produced ingots which were one gram light. The customs officers became aware of this fraud from an undercover agent and set about trying to find the light ingots.

In their bonded warehouse at the time they had several consignments of 100 ingots each made up of 10 piles of 10 ingots. Their information told them that one pile of 10 ingots in each consignment came from the dishonest exporter and they wanted to find an efficient way of finding the light pile in each consignment. After some thought a customs officer came up with a neat method which enabled them to find the light pile in each consignment using just one weighing. How was it done?

32   Billy Bunter's bargain

Billy Bunter was delighted when the manufacturer of
SCRUNCH, his favourite chocolate bar, decided to have a
special promotion for a limited period. They authorised the
shopkeepers to give a bar, free, to anyone presenting them
with eight SCRUNCH labels.

   Billy persuaded all his friends to donate their labels to him,
and by the end of the period he had collected 71 labels.

   How many free SCRUNCH bars was Billy able to collect
at his school tuckshop?

33   All touching

Show how to arrange six pencils (or matchsticks) so that each
of them is touching the other five.

34 Mechanism miscellany

The study of mechanisms took off in the nineteenth century following the great interest aroused by finding mechanical solutions to straight-line motion. Tchebycheff 1821–94, a distinguished Russian mathematician, whose solution was discussed in *Mathematical Activities*, was so fascinated by this new way of approaching spatial problems that in writing to the British mathematician Sylvester, he encouraged him to concentrate on the study of mechanisms rather than geometry. The former, he believed, had much more to offer and would also add a fourth dimension (motion) to space. Sylvester became as enthusiastic as Tchebycheff and did much to promote this new subject (kinematics) by lecturing widely and demonstrating mechanisms, particularly those which produced straight-line motion. One result of his lectures was an improved design for a large air pump to improve the ventilation in the House of Commons!

One of the first solutions to the straight-line motion problem was put forward by Cartwright, the inventor of the mechanical loom. In 1800 he patented the mechanism illustrated in (a). Two cranks, *A* and *B*, are geared so that they turn symmetrically at the same speed in opposite directions. The cranks are linked by connecting rods to the bar *CD* whose mid-point *M* is attached to the piston rod and ensures that it moves in a straight line.

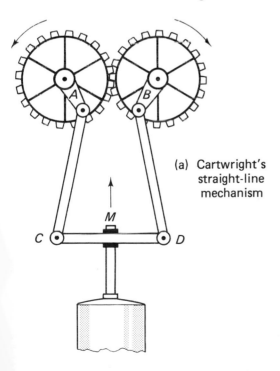

(a) Cartwright's straight-line mechanism

Everyone is familiar with the to and fro motion of a car windscreen wiper. This motion can be achieved quite simply from a constant speed motor by a mechanism like that shown in (b). As A travels in a circle around D the rod AB oscillates the rod CB about the point C. This mechanism is widely used in industrial processes where an agitator is required just as in the agitator of many domestic washing machines.

But look now at diagrams (c) and (d).

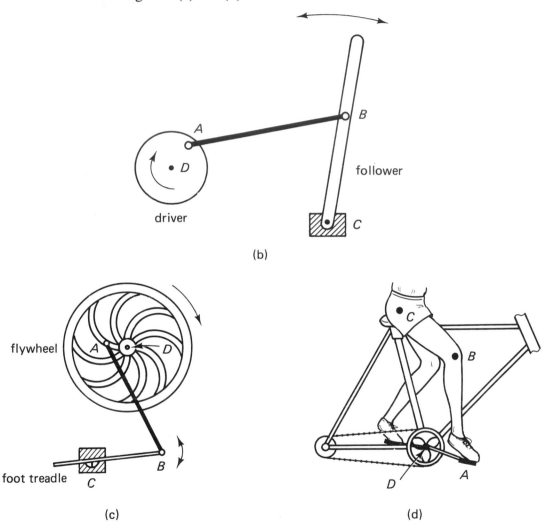

(b)

flywheel

foot treadle

(c)

(d)

The first shows the treadle mechanism familiar on old sewing machines and spinning wheels. This is essentially the same as the previous mechanism but now the rod BC is the driver and the flywheel is the follower. With the cyclist two bars BC and BA of the mechanism are replaced by the cyclist's leg, while the pedal crank AD makes complete revolutions about D. When analysed, these three situations can all be seen as examples of a 4-bar linkage $ABCD$ in which AD revolves about D and BC 'rocks' about C, see (e).

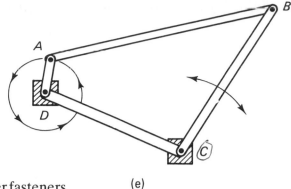

(e)

Make a 4-bar linkage using card strips and paper fasteners and investigate the angle turned through by BC as AD makes complete revolutions.

Design a suitable mechanism to give the correct sweep for a windscreen wiper or to model a cyclist.

The oscillating mechanisms discussed so far have all been symmetric in the sense that they have taken as long to move in one direction as the other. The mechanism illustrated in (f) however has been designed to give a slow feed and quick return. As the flywheel is driven with constant speed about D, a pin A near its circumference slides along the slot in bar CB making this bar oscillate about C. However, as (g) shows, the pin A spends a much longer part of one revolution pushing B to the left than it does returning B to the right. If the acute angle MDN is 60° for example then CB moves from its extreme left position CB_L to its extreme right position CB_R in one fifth of the time it takes to go from CB_R to CB_L. Such a mechanism is used in a joiner's shop where B is attached to a cutting blade which does work in one direction but not the other, as in planing wood.

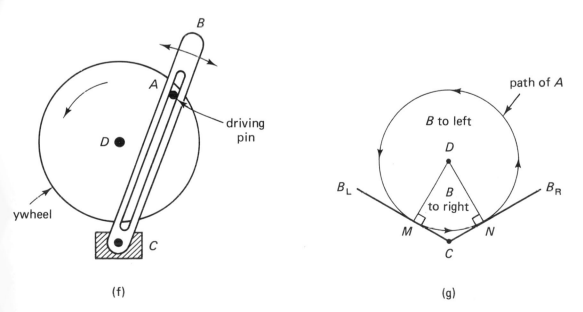

(f)

(g)

An ingenious mechanism is that seen on older sewing machines whose purpose is to feed cotton evenly onto a spool when it is being rewound, so cotton is fed onto the spool over the cotton guide which needs to move from left to right at a constant speed in order that the cotton is wound evenly over the whole width of the spool.

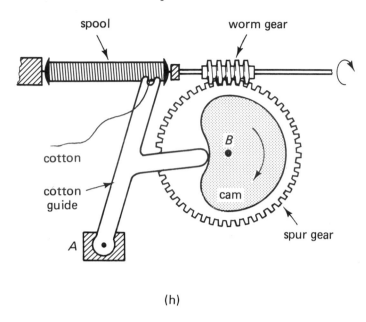

(h)

In the mechanism illustrated a worm gear, on the shaft which turns the spool, engages a spur gear which turns slowly about B. Attached to the spur gear is a raised shape (a cam), not unlike a cardioid, which pushes against the cotton guide and moves it along the length of the spool. A spring always ensures that the cotton guide is pressed against the cam, and the number of teeth on the spur wheel determines how many winds of cotton go onto the spool as the cotton guide moves once across it.

Try to get a close look at an old sewing machine which has this mechanism and observe it in operation. Better still investigate all the mechanisms on a sewing machine. Try to see what their purpose is and how it has been achieved.

35   Patchwork patterns

To anyone familiar with patchwork designs the one shown here called 'Baby's blocks' is sure to be known. By using three different coloured materials and one rhombic template, equivalent to two equilateral triangles, the pieces can be sewn together as shown to produce a tantalising

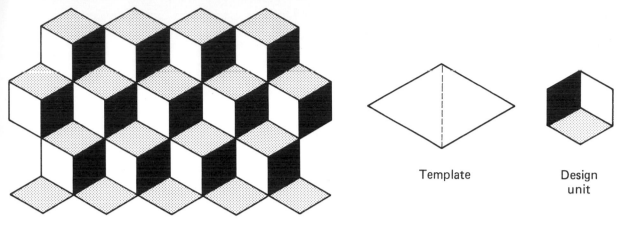

Template

Design
unit

Baby's blocks

three-dimensional effect of solid cubes. In fact you can
probably see the cubes in two ways – what appears to be a
cube thrusting towards you at one instance is a cubical space
going away from you the next. Because of the three colours
used the design unit is a hexagon made up of one rhombus of
each colour.

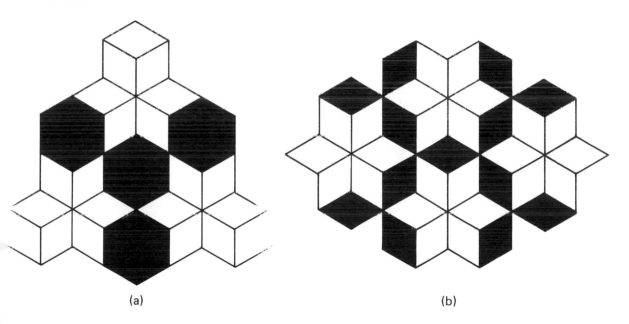

(a)

(b)

From the basic rhombic tessellation many different designs
can be achieved just by the way the different colour materials
are used. The two star designs, see (a) and (b), have been
achieved by using just two colours and varying the
proportions of each used. Because the design is more
complex than the Baby's block pattern the design units are
larger, see (c) and (d). In (c) there is an equal proportion of
each colour, but in (d) there is twice as much white as black.

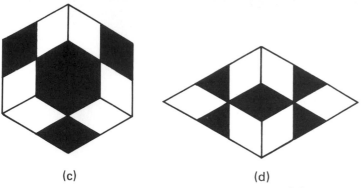

(c)   (d)

The basic design unit is the smallest area of the pattern which, if repeated, would produce the whole pattern. The areas selected in (c) and (d) are not the only ones which would produce designs (a) and (b) but are probably the easiest to see.

Looking at the Baby's blocks design very carefully you can just about see the star patterns if you concentrate, but the effect of the colouring makes it very difficult.

Many patchwork designs use more than one basic shape to achieve their effect and often employ squares and the triangles formed by dividing a square by a diagonal. Some of these are shown below.

Broken dishes

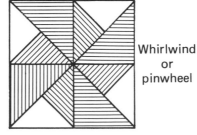

The wrench

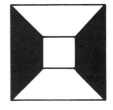

Milky way

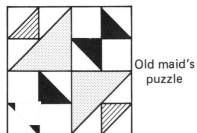

Old maid's puzzle

Whirlwind or pinwheel

Spool

The design unit may or may not be interesting in itself but when placed side by side with copies of itself intriguing designs can appear which can be very appealing. Kaleidoscope and Arabic lattice illustrate this point. The unit for Kaleidoscope seems to be a simple 4-pointed star but the overall pattern is a beautiful design of interlocking stars.

Unit of
design

Kaleidoscope

A

B

Unit of
design

Arabic lattice

The unit for Arabic lattice doesn't begin to suggest the interlocking almost frog-like shapes of the overall design which is reminiscent of some of Escher's work.

To achieve the Kaleidoscope pattern the small block given needs to be *rotated* as well as translated so strictly speaking it is not the basic unit. The true basic unit needs to contain four of these small blocks, one in each of the orientations in which it occurs in the patterns. Such a block would be one of the corner squares formed by cutting the large pattern into four, or the square in the centre which contains the complete black 4-pointed star. Similarly, with the Arabic lattice the blocks *A* and *B* which are mirror images are both needed and the true basic unit is again the square formed by quartering the large pattern given.

Try drawing some of these patterns and designing some of your own. You do not need to make them into patchwork to obtain pleasure from them. One approach would be to cut out the triangles and squares from coloured card or paper and fit them together like a jigsaw.

When drawing these patterns it is very helpful to start with a sheet of squared paper – 1 cm squared paper is a good size to use. The sequence of diagrams below show how to obtain the basic shapes for the Kaleidoscope and Arabic lattice.

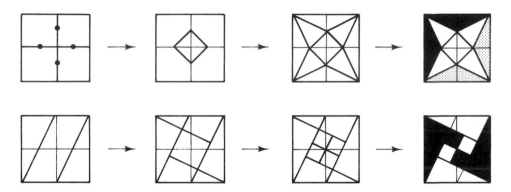

There are many traditional designs with names such as Crazy Ann, Spider Web, Goose Tracks, Jacob's Ladder, Jack in the Box, etc. to be investigated. Dover Publications publish a number of very practical, well-illustrated books on patchwork design with titles such as *101 Patchwork Patterns* and *Geometric Patchwork Patterns* which are full of ideas.

36 Fun with subtraction

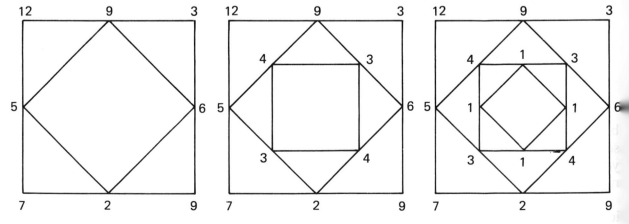

Start by drawing a square. Put a number at each vertex (12, 7, 9 and 3 are used above), then draw a new square inside the first square by joining the mid-points of its sides.

A number is now allocated to each vertex of the new square by finding the difference between the numbers at the ends of the line on which it stands (e.g. $12 - 7 = 5, 9 - 7 = 2$, $9 - 3 = 6$ and $12 - 3 = 9$). The square just formed is taken as the starting point and the process continued until all the numbers at the vertices of a square are the same.

Because the new set of numbers at each stage corresponds to the gaps between the previous numbers they will be reducing in size so the process must either end after a finite number of steps, or the pattern of numbers will start to repeat. How many steps are required until one of these happens?

The example shown above required three steps, the one below requires five steps.

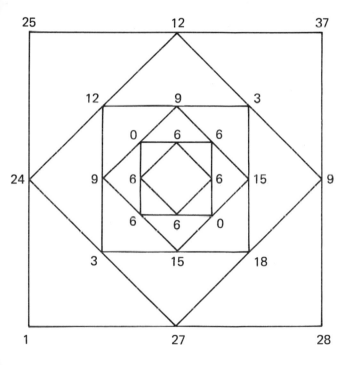

Limit the size of the numbers you start with, to say, 25, to begin with and investigate what happens. What is the longest sequence of squares you can find with this limitation? Can you obtain a sequence with more steps by using larger numbers to start with?

Observe carefully the way the final stages produce four identical numbers at the vertices.

See if you can build up a sequence of squares in reverse by starting with the square in the middle having the numbers at its vertices identical.

37 Gale

This is a game devised by David Gale who was a professor of mathematics at Brown University. The playing area consists of two rectangles of intermeshed dots. In the area shown the rectangles are both 6 × 5 and one set of dots is shown as crosses to make them distinguishable. Player *A* tries to make a continuous path between side *a* and side *a'* joining the crosses, while player *B* tries to make a continuous path between side *b* and side *b'* joining the dots.

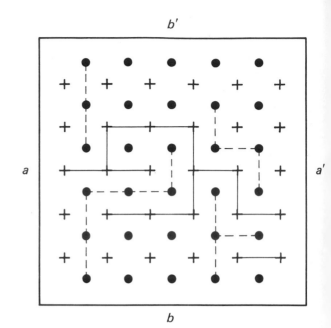

Players take turns to join any pair of adjacent dots or crosses, with vertical or horizontal, but not diagonal, lines. Paths may not cross!

The board shows the end of a game won by *A*.

You may recognise the game as having similarities to Hex which was described in *Mathematical Activities*, but there the whole playing surface was available to both players unlike this game where the staging posts are necessarily disjoint.

38 Guess the number

This is a number guessing game which stems from Mastermind.

  A thinks of a 2-digit number
  B makes a guess at the number
  A then makes one of 4 responses

(1) ✗ which implies neither digit is correct
(2) ✓ which implies one digit correct but in the wrong place
(3) * which implies one digit correct and in the right place
(4) ✓✓ which implies both digits correct but the wrong way around.

B needs to keep a record of the guesses with *A*'s responses so that the later guesses are better informed.

This game can be played by a teacher writing up guesses and responses on the board initially, but it is better played between two individuals who switch roles after each game and compare the number of guesses required to find the number.

39 Trackwords

For many weeks the *Radio Times* set a word puzzle based on
a 3 × 3 square. Readers were challenged to find a nine-letter
word by tracking from a letter to an adjacent letter going up,
down, across or diagonally as a king's move in chess. An
example of such a puzzle is shown here. See if you can find
the word.

Y	I	D
R	V	S
E	C	O

If you try to find the word blindly without using your
experience of which letters are likely to come next to each
other you could be in for a long search. There are many
potential nine letter 'words' in such an array. The real puzzle
is to find exactly how many ways you could trace a path
through the nine letters in the array.

Alternatively you can think of the problem as that of
finding how many different king's tours are possible on a
3 × 3 chessboard.

40 Toasting efficiently

An old-fashioned electric toaster is only capable of toasting
one side each of two pieces of bread at the same time.

Two hands are needed to insert, remove and turn each
slice.

The time to toast a side is 30 seconds; the time to turn over
a slice is 2 seconds; the time to remove a slice and put it on a
plate or to take a slice from the plate and put it in the toaster
is 3 seconds. Starting with three slices of bread on a plate,
find the minimum time to get three slices of toast on the
plate.

41 The prime gaps

Counting from 1 to 100 it is not far from one prime number to
the next, but as you count on past 100 some of the gaps from
one prime to the next are surprisingly large. Between 1000
and 2000 for example there are five gaps of 20 or more.
Investigate!

42   Always one short

479 has the interesting property that when it is:

> divided by 6 it leaves a remainder of 5,
> divided by 5 it leaves a remainder of 4,
> divided by 4 it leaves a remainder of 3,
> divided by 3 it leaves a remainder of 2,
> divided by 2 it leaves a remainder of 1.

Which is the smallest number with this property?

There are three numbers less than 10 000 with the property that on division by 10, 9, 8, 7, 6, 5, 4, 3 and 2 the remainder left is always one less than the number divided by. Can you find them?

43   Truncating primes

The number 73 939 133 has the fascinating property that not only is it prime, but as the least significant digit is successively chopped off the remaining numbers are also prime, namely

> 7 393 913,   739 391,   73 939,   7393,   739,   73,   7.

Incidentally this number is the largest with this property. In all there are 83 such numbers. Can you find them?

To set you on your search the tree diagram below shows how you might find all such numbers beginning with 2. It includes all the possible numbers beginning with 2 which have 4 or fewer digits, namely

> 2,   23,   233,   2333,   2339,   239,   2393,   2399,
> 29,   293,   2939.

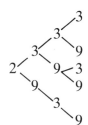

Some interesting patterns arise such as 23, 233, 2333, 23333 which are all prime and may tempt you into assuming that 3s could be added ad infinitum, but be warned,

$$233\,333 = 353 \times 661.$$

A table of prime numbers and a calculator will take you a long way with this investigation, but for the larger numbers use a program on a micro which can test a number to see if it is a prime.

44   The tournament draw

For the end of season squash tournament there were 27
entries. The tournament was arranged on a knockout basis
with the loser of each match being eliminated. A number of
players received a bye in the first round so that from the
second round onwards the number of players going forward
at each stage was halved.

   Norman and Theresa, the squash captains, met to arrange
the draw. Their first problem was to decide how many
matches would be needed in the first round and hence how
many players should have byes. Norman was worried, he
didn't really know how to begin, but Theresa with experience
of organising tennis tournaments on similar lines was very
quickly able to say how many rounds would be needed, how
many byes to give and how many matches there would be in
the whole tournament. What are the numbers involved?

   How many matches would need to be played in a
tournament with N players?

45   The police officer's beat

The map shows the streets which have to be patrolled by a
police officer on the beat. The length of side of a small square
represents 100 m, and the total length of road to be patrolled
is 2.5 km. What is the shortest distance the police officer can
walk to patrol the whole beat?

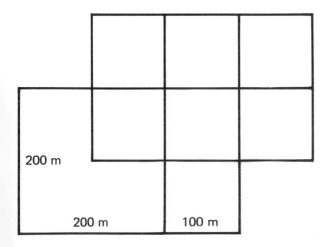

200 m

200 m   100 m

46 Coincident birthdays

Dr P Are, the headmaster of a large comprehensive school, noticed that in more than half of all the classes there were at least two children whose birthdays coincided. He argued to himself that as there are 365 days in a year, a class would have to have 366 children to be certain of having two children with the same birthday.

Now he knew that the average class size was 30 in his school, so he reckoned that all those coinciding birthdays must be a record. Always one for publicity he was all for writing to the newspapers and the *Guiness Book of Records*. Luckily for him, however, his colleague Angie Analysis heard of his ambitions and stopped him making a fool of himself by showing him that the coincidences were to be expected. What argument did she use? What is the probability of a class of 30 having at least two people with the same birthday?

47 The Embassy reception

There were 80 ambassadors at the Utopian Embassy's reception. By the end of the evening every one of the ambassadors had been formally introduced and shaken hands with every other ambassador. How many handshakes took place?

48 Narcissistic numbers

The number 153 has the interesting property that it is equal to the sum of the cubes of its digits.

$$1^3 + 5^3 + 3^3 = 1 + 125 + 27 = 153$$

370 is another number with the same property.
   Ignoring unity, there are two further numbers, both less than 500 with the same property. Can you find them?

49   Getting to know the octahedron

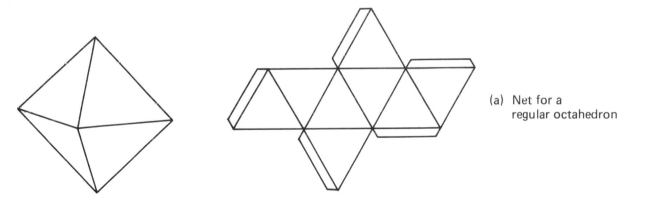

(a) Net for a regular octahedron

The name octahedron comes from the Greek words *octo* meaning eight and *hedron* meaning facet. Here we are going to look especially at the regular octahedron which has eight equilateral triangle faces. Each vertex has four triangles meeting at it and is the same as every other vertex. Make an octahedron using an enlargement of net (a). A length of 8 cm for the edge of the triangle gives a good-sized model and fits onto a piece of A4 paper or card. If you make the model using card be sure to score each line to be folded to get a good edge.

(b)

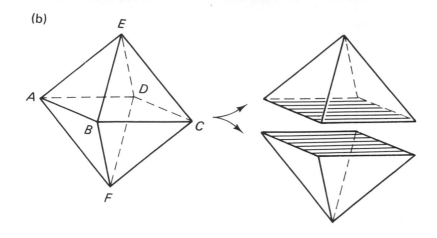

An octahedron can be looked at in many different ways, each of which tells us more about it. Constructing the model from a net concentrates the attention on the shape of the faces, and the number which meet at a vertex. However, when you handle the model other aspects become apparent. Imagine cutting the solid in half with a horizontal slice through the vertices A, B, C and D, see (b). The effect of this is to divide the solid into two identical square-based pyramids. The same effect would also result if the octahedron was turned so that any other vertex such as A or B was held at the top. In fact, if the octahedron was not marked in any way it would be impossible to tell one vertex from another – or for that matter, any face from another.

Because of this symmetry, any slice half-way between a pair of opposite vertices gives a square cross-section as shown in (c).

(c)

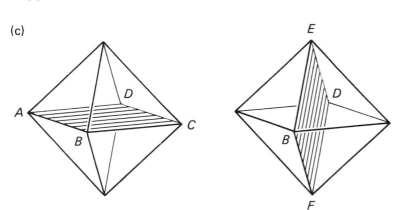
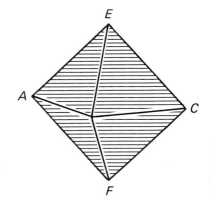

This gives us a new way of looking at an octahedron and suggests a different way of making a model.

Cut out two squares from card to represent the cross-sections $ABCD$ and $EBFD$. Cut slots in these squares as shown in (d) and slot them together along BOD.

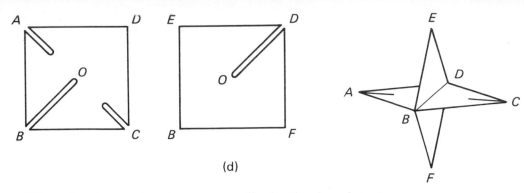

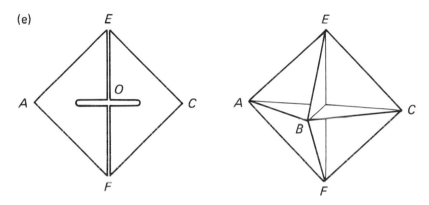

(d)

When the pieces of card are perpendicular the six points A, B, C, D, E and F are at the vertices of a regular octahedron.

To complete the model, cut out a third square to represent $AECF$. Cut it in half along diagonal EF and make slots along the lines OA and OC as shown in (e). Now add these half squares to complete the model and use glue or sticky tape to keep it together.

(e)

Another way of making a model that emphasises the square cross-sections of the regular octahedron uses three wire squares. (Try using old wire coat hangers and painting them different colours.) Join them at their corners by tying with thread. This model emphasises the edges of the octahedron.

This edge model can also be made by threading straws onto lengths of thread or shirring elastic and tying the ends. However, when using straws it is usual to start with a triangle and then build further triangles onto it until the model is complete. But it is quite instructive to make three separate loops of four straws to represent $ABCD$, $ACEF$ and $BEDF$ and then join them – until the last join is made the model will have no in-built rigidity.

Starting from one vertex of an octahedron, say A, it is possible to find a route along all its edges and return to the starting point without having to retrace any edge, for example

(f)

$$A \rightarrow B \rightarrow E \rightarrow D \rightarrow F \rightarrow B \rightarrow C \rightarrow D \rightarrow A \rightarrow E \rightarrow C \rightarrow F \rightarrow A$$

H.E. Dudney once set a puzzle based on this idea. He challenged his readers to find just how many such paths there are from one vertex. The number is surprisingly large. See if you can find it.

The fact that such a path exists means you could make a straw octahedron by first making a closed loop of twelve straws. Try doing it this way!

(g)

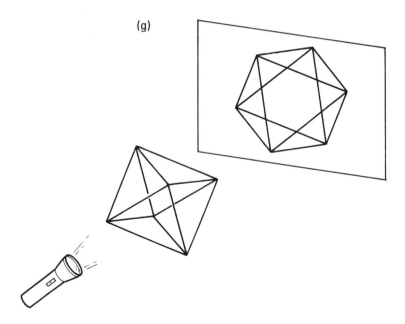

If a straw octahedron is held in front of a screen and a torch shone through it a wide variety of shadows can be formed, but the most surprising is that of a hexagon with its diagonals. How is this obtained?

With straw models it is easy to add on a tetrahedron by adding three extra straws to a triangular face. If you start with

an octahedron and add four such tetrahedrons to alternate
faces the result is a larger tetrahedron.

(h)

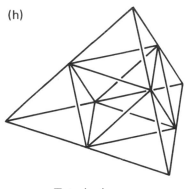
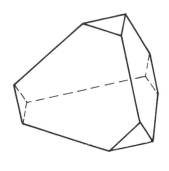
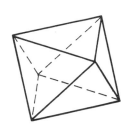

| Tetrahedron | Truncated tetrahedron | Octahedron as limit of truncation |

Another way to see this relationship between a regular
tetrahedron and a regular octahedron is to truncate a regular
tetrahedron by cutting off its corners symmetrically; see (h).

If, again, the octahedron is taken as a starting point and a
tetrahedron is added to each of its eight faces the result can
be seen as an 8-pointed star, or as two interlocking
tetrahedrons whose common middle is the original
octahedron; see (i).

(i)

Two interlocking
tetrahedrons

(j)

(k)

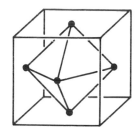

Now take a closer look at the 8-pointed star and you will
see that the points are at the vertices of a cube (j), and
furthermore, the original octahedron has its vertices at the
centres of the cube's faces (k).

This close relationship between a cube and an octahedron
is even more marked. If the octahedron is taken as starting
point and lines are drawn joining the mid-points of its
adjacent faces then a cube is formed (l). Because of this the
cube and the octahedron are said to be *dual* and their
symmetry is identical. Any plane of symmetry for the cube is

(l)

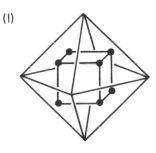

49

a plane of symmetry for the octahedron. Similarly with axes of rotational symmetry. The limiting shape produced by truncating either the cube or the octahedron is also the same and, not surprisingly, is called a cuboctahedron, see (m).

(m)
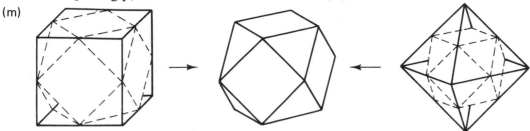

Crystals occur naturally in these shapes; for example, common salt crystals are cubical, alum crystals occur as octahedrons, and argentite, a mineral of silver, is found as cuboctahedron crystals. This is not really surprising when we see the different ways in which spheres can pack together to fill space. The following diagrams show the most obvious

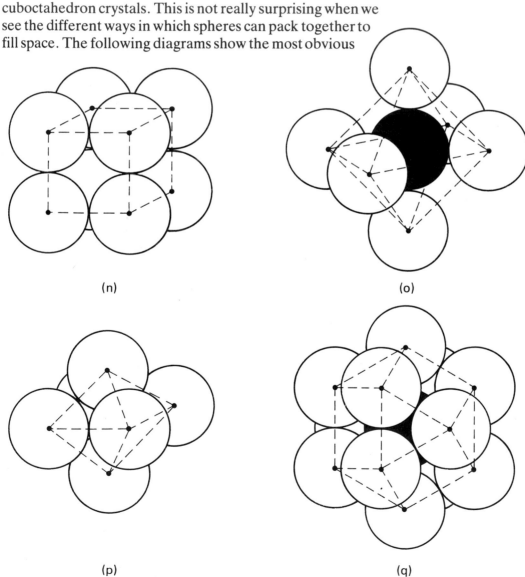

(n)

(o)

(p)

(q)

ways and their link with these shapes. But really to
appreciate this it helps to make models using spheres of
polystyrene beads or marbles.

In (n) and (o) the spheres are packed in a square pattern on
each layer with each new layer identical. This is known as
cubical packing and is exemplified by (n). However, if one
considers the six spheres touching any given sphere, see (o),
their centres lie at the vertices of a regular octahedron. The
octahedron is again apparent when each layer of spheres is in
a square pattern but the spheres for each new layer lie in the
hollows of the previous layer, see (p). The cuboctahedron
can be seen when each layer forms hexagonal patterns and
the new layers sit in alternate hollows formed by the previous
layer see (q). Also note that in this case every other layer is
such that the spheres are not immediately above one another
but correspond to the hollows in the middle layer left by the
other.

50   The stamp machine

A stamp machine was being designed so that in return for a
20p coin and a 10p coin it would eject a strip of stamps worth
30p. To gain publicity the Post Office decided to hold a
competition. The public were asked to suggest the values for
the individual stamps in a strip, so that any letter or package
could be stamped correctly with sums from 1p to 30p.

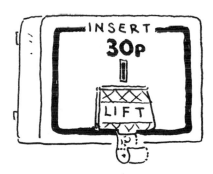

In the end they awarded two first prizes of free postage for
a year, one to Mrs Royale Mail and the other to the Rev
Énue. Mrs Royale Mail had shown that the problem could be
solved with a strip of just five stamps, and her solution was
eventually used.

What were the values of the five stamps?

The Rev Énue, however, had found a solution where any
of the values from 1p to 30p could be found by using a single
stamp or a *connected* set of stamps. One way to do this would
be to have a strip of thirty 1p stamps but you can do a lot
better than that! What is the smallest number of stamps
which could be used to achieve this, and what will be their
values and order on the strip?

51 Investigating books of postage stamps

(*a*) The cost of postage for letters of different mass to different parts of the world varies considerably. To give a 24-hour service to customers requiring postage stamps the GPO place machines outside their main post offices which dispense a book of eight stamps for 50p.

The problem for the post office is to decide what values to give the eight stamps so that they can be used for as many different situations as possible. In the summer of 1985, for example, the following rates applied.

Inland letters	60 g	100 g	150 g	200 g
1st class	17p	24p	31p	38p
2nd class	13p	18p	22p	28p

Overseas air letters	10 g	20 g
Middle East	29p	40p
Africa	31p	45p
Australia	34p	49p

Aerogrammes 26p
Overseas postcards 22p and 37p.

With such a range of rates, deciding on the stamp values for the book presents an interesting problem. What values would you give to the eight stamps? Compare your solution with that of the GPO given in the commentary.

On the day when this was written the GPO announced a reduction in the rate of 2nd class letters from 13p to 12p to celebrate their 350th anniversary. How would you modify your solution to take this into account?

Find the current postage rates and design a suitable 50p book.

(*b*) One GPO stamp designer, more out of curiosity than practicality, decided to try a different but related problem. The aim was to design a book with six stamps in a 3×2 page in such a way that by removing a single stamp or a connected set of stamps it would be possible to match all possible postage rates 1p, 2p, 3p, ..., Np where N was to be as large as possible. There would be no conditions on the values of stamps which were allowed and the first solution is shown

here. The designer was very pleased with it to start with for it seemed possible to tear off a stamp or a connected set of stamps for all values from 1p to 32p. However, on checking there was one value which could not be made up. (Note that the stamps must be connected by their edges.)

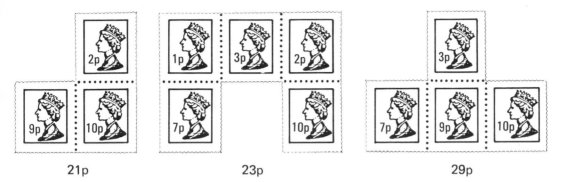

21p   23p   29p

The diagram shows connected sets of stamps which give totals of 21p, 23p and 29p respectively. Check all the other totals from 1p to 32p and find which one is not possible.

Eventually the designer found values for the stamps which made it possible to get further than 32p and without any gaps. How far can you get?

52 Designing an efficient ruler

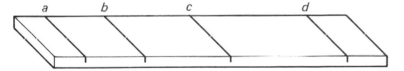

Reflecting on the cluttered markings on a ruler, a carpenter observed that if there were four saw-cuts on a piece of wood such as a, b, c and d (see diagram) there would be six gaps between them, namely ab, ac, ad, bc, bd and cd. By suitably spacing the cuts the gaps could be arranged to be 1 cm, 2 cm, 3 cm, 4 cm, 5 cm and 6 cm in some order.

Show how this could be done.

By making five saw-cuts the carpenter realised there would be ten gaps, but was unable to space them to correspond to gaps of 1 cm, 2 cm, ..., 10 cm.

What is the best you can do with five saw-cuts?

Investigate the number of gaps between different numbers of saw-cuts and see if you can find a rule connecting them.

Further, investigate the gaps to leave between the cuts to make it possible to measure lengths of 1 cm, 2 cm, ..., n cm, where n is as large as possible.

53 Number the sectors

Find numbers A, B, C, D, E, and F for the six sectors so that the number in a sector, or the total of the numbers in a set of adjacent sectors, gives all the integers from 1 to 25 inclusive.

Is it possible to obtain a larger range of numbers in this way?

Investigate the numbers required to give the largest range of totals when the circle is divided into 2, 3, 4, 5, ..., n sectors.

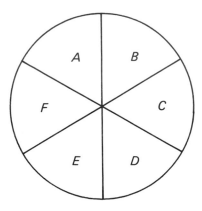

54 Three of a kind

Some games which, on the face of it have nothing in common turn out to be structurally identical. The following games for two players form such a group.

1 Take a pack of playing cards and from it extract the ace and 2 to 9 of diamonds. Lay these nine cards face upwards on the table and, with ace counting as 1, players in turn pick a card from the table. The first person to hold *three* cards which total 15 is the winner.

2 Print each of the nine words on a card as shown and place them face up on the table.

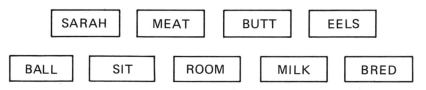

Players, in turn, pick a card off the table. The first person to hold *three* cards containing the same letter wins.

3 The game of Jam devised by the Dutch psychologist J.A.
Michon is based on a map consisting of 9 motorways
joining 8 towns as shown. Some of the motorways pass
through one or more towns while others just join adjacent
towns.

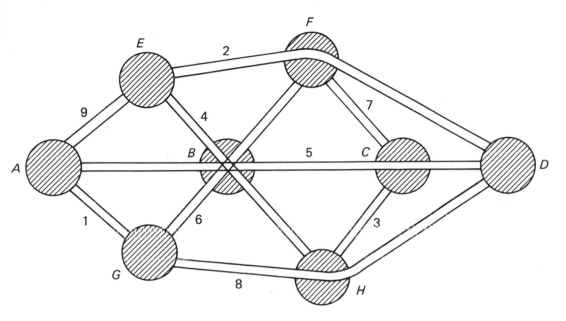

Players play alternately and, using coloured pencils,
colour in one of the motorways at each turn. A player wins
by colouring *three* motorways to the same town.

First try playing these games and when you think you know
what they are all about see if you can show the connection
between them.

What other well-known game has a similar structure?
Now look at the commentary!

55   Rearranging the hospital ward

A hospital ward contains 16 beds as shown. Using eight
screens the ward has been subdivided into four regions
containing 8, 3, 3 and 2 beds respectively, categorised by the
patients' illnesses. With a new intake it is necessary to
subdivide the ward into three regions containing 6, 6 and 4
beds.

What is the smallest number of screens that could be
moved to achieve this?

56 Tangrams

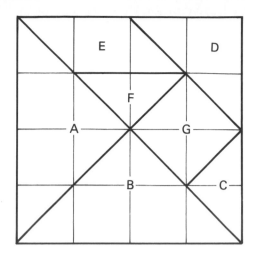

Start with a square piece of card (8 cm × 8 cm is a convenient size) and cut it into the seven pieces shown.

Now try fitting the pieces together to form the shapes below. Note all seven pieces must be used.

This is an ancient Chinese puzzle which is ageless.

The shapes shown below are just a sample of the hundreds of possible ones. The book by van Delft and Botermans, *Creative Puzzles of the World*, is an excellent reference on this puzzle, known as a tangram, and of many others such as circular and egg-shaped tangrams.

57　Make a century

$$96 + \frac{2148}{537} = 100$$

There are eleven ways in which the digits 1, 2, …, 9 can be arranged as a whole number plus a rational number whose sum is 100. One of these ways is shown above. See how many of the others you can find.

58　Mixed doubles

The village tennis club was quite a modest affair having only two courts. On one Saturday afternoon only eight players turned up to play,

　　Adrian, Bernard, Colin, David
　　Amanda, Brenda, Carole and Doris.

　Carole, the club secretary, always ready to organise, soon proposed a plan for mixed doubles. Her plan envisaged everyone playing three matches in such a way that no one ever had the same partner twice or the same opponent twice. The ingenuity of this plan pleased everyone so it was readily accepted.

　What was Carole's plan?

59 Ever more triangles and squares

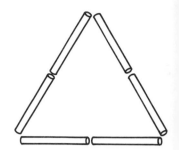

Take six drinking straws and cut them in half to give twelve short straws. Arrange them to make the two equilateral triangles shown.

How else could you make two equilateral triangles using all of the short straws?

Using all twelve of your short straws in each case show how to make:

(a) one equilateral triangle
(b) three equilateral triangles
(c) four equilateral triangles
(d) five equilateral triangles
(e) six equilateral triangles
(f) eight equilateral triangles
(g) one square
(h) two squares
(i) three squares
(j) five squares
(k) six squares
(l) three squares and eight triangles

What other arrangements can you make using all the straws?

60 Pythagoras revisited

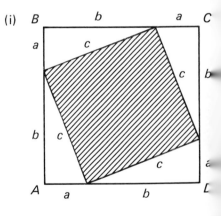

(i)

The demonstration of Pythagoras' theorem known as Perigal's dissection was described in *Mathematical Activities* (activity 64), but as it is such an important theorem the opportunity is being taken here to put together some of the more accessible demonstrations and proofs of it for comparison.

The first three of these are very similar and as a starting point require four identical right-angled triangles. Cut them out of card and see it as a practical activity.

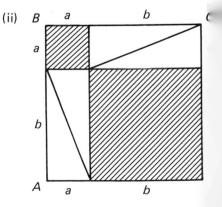

(ii)

1 Place the four triangles as shown in (i) to form a square *ABCD* of side $a + b$ and leaving a square hole (shaded) of side c in the middle.

Draw in the square *ABCD*. Now move the triangles to take up the position shown in (ii), which leaves two square holes of sides a and b. The shaded area must be the same in each case, so

$$c^2 = a^2 + b^2$$

2 This proof is based on diagram (i) above:

area of square $ABCD$ = area of shaded square + area of 4 triangles

so $\qquad (a+b)^2 = c^2 + 4 \times (\tfrac{1}{2}ab)$

from which $\quad a^2 + b^2 = c^2$

3 This time arrange the four triangles with their right angles inwards so that they all lie inside a square $PQRS$ of side c. The hole in the centre (shaded) is now a square of side $b-a$.

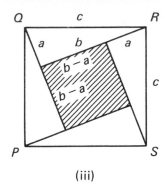

(iii)

area of square $PQRS$ = area of shaded square + area of 4 triangles

so $\qquad c^2 = (b-a)^2 + 4 \times (\tfrac{1}{2}ab)$

from which $\qquad c^2 = a^2 + b^2$

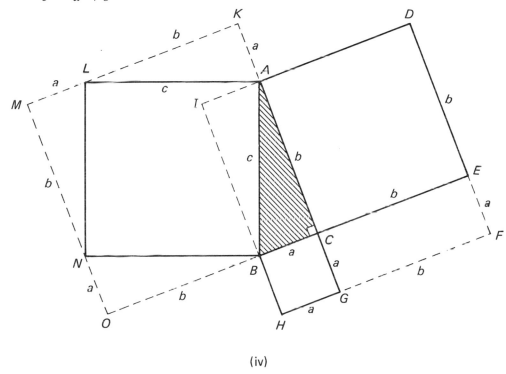

(iv)

4 This proof was first published in 1860 and again depends on matching equivalent areas. It will be seen to have many similarities to the first two above.

area of square $ABNL$
  = area of square $KCOM$ – area of 4 triangles
  = area of square $DFHI$ – area of 4 triangles
  = area of square $DFHI$ – area $ACBI$ – area $CEFG$
  = area $ADEC$ + area $BCGH$

thus

$\qquad c^2 = b^2 + a^2$

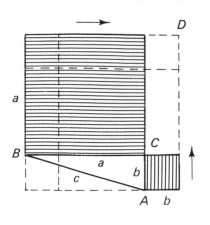
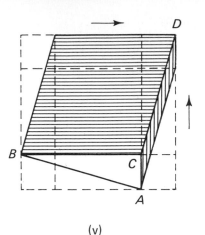
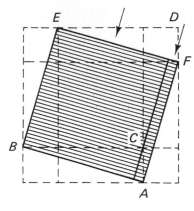

(v)

5 With the introduction of transformation geometry to many
syllabuses, the proof shown here based on the shearing
transformation is interesting. See (v).

The square on BC is sheared to the right and the square
on AC is sheared up to meet along the line CD.
(Remember the shearing transformation keeps area
invariant.) The resulting parallelograms are now sheared
in the direction of DC until they meet BA and together
form the square $ABEF$.

Hence
    area of square on AB = area of square on BC + area of
                              square on AC

so $c^2 = a^2 + b^2$

6 A proof which is sometimes explained using similar
triangles but is more easily expressed using
trigonometrical functions is based on (vi).

$$AB = AN + NB$$
$$c \;\; = b \cos \theta + a \cos \phi \qquad \text{(vi)}$$
$$c \;\; = b . \frac{b}{c} + a . \frac{a}{c}$$

as $\cos \theta = \dfrac{b}{c}$ and $\cos \phi = \dfrac{a}{c}$ from $\triangle ABC$,

which on multiplying through by c again gives
$$c^2 = b^2 + a^2$$

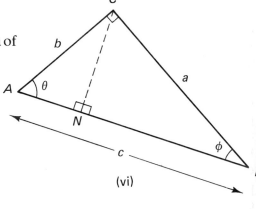

7 One of the most satisfying proofs of the theorem is that
which results from the use of vectors. See (vii).

$$c^2 = \mathbf{c} . \mathbf{c}$$
$$= (\mathbf{a} + \mathbf{b}) . (\mathbf{a} + \mathbf{b})$$
$$= \mathbf{a} . \mathbf{a} + 2\mathbf{a} . \mathbf{b} + \mathbf{b} . \mathbf{b}$$
$$= a^2 + b^2$$

as $\mathbf{a} . \mathbf{b} = 0$ when $\mathbf{a} \perp \mathbf{b}$.

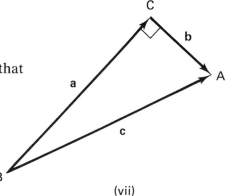

(vii)

61 The Maltese cross mechanism

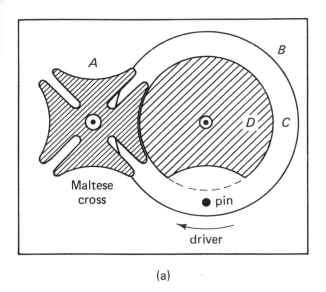

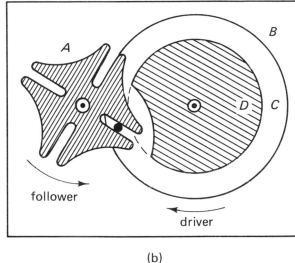

(a) (b)

For a cine camera or a cine projector to work the film has to
be pulled through intermittently. A frame is held still in front
of the lens while a photo is taken, or an image projected and
then it is rapidly jerked on to the next frame, held still, jerked
on, etc. The driver in each case is a constant speed motor, so
how can it produce such an intermittent stop–start motion?
The answer is in the ingenious mechanism illustrated here
based on the shape of a Maltese cross, A. Wheel B consists of
a large disc C with a smaller raised disc D fixed to it which
prevents the Maltese cross from turning for most of the time,
as in (a). However, part of disc D is cut away at one point and
this coincides with a pin that sticks up from C and engages in
one of the slots of the cross A as disc C turns. In doing so the
pin flicks the cross A through 90° and then holds it still until
disc C has made another revolution and the pin engages in
the next slot of the cross.

This model can be made with a little patience if you have
suitable tools. Disc C and cross A could be cut from a plastic
box such as an ice cream container, but disc D needs to be a
thicker material and is best cut from hardboard or plywood.
A few nuts and bolts and washers complete the model, and a
longer pin attached to D, diametrically opposite to the pin
which engages in A, can be added as a handle to manipulate
the model.

62　The geometry of rotary pumps

As soon as a car engine is started pumps come into play to deliver petrol to the carburettor, circulate the water in the cooling system and to pump oil to lubricate the engine. The blower which delivers hot or cold air into the car is yet another pump of a sort, as is the blower in the domestic vacuum cleaner. In the modern home too the water will be circulated around the central heating system, the cooling fluid around the deep freeze and the washing machine emptied of soapy water by rotary pumps. But you have probably never given them a thought!

The principle behind the working of most rotary pumps is best illustrated by a vane pump. A cross-section of such a pump is given in (a). As the rotor turns about a fixed axis it makes close contact with the pump casing between the inlet and outlet channels. Fitted into the rotor are two vanes which are constantly pushed out to make contact with the casing by a spring between them.

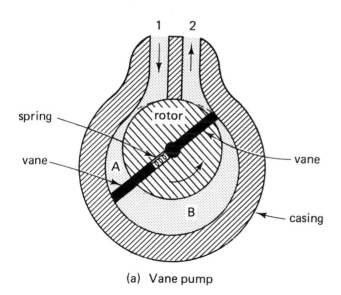

(a)　Vane pump

With the rotor in the position shown, air is being drawn in through channel 1 to fill the space A. The space B containing air is cut off from both inlet and outlet channels but will soon be connected to the outlet 2, and as the rotor rotates, all the air which was contained in B will be pushed out through channel 2. What was space A becomes a new space B as the top vane moves past channel 1, and the cycle keeps repeating itself.

Pumps like this can be very efficient and are used to evacuate air from vacuum tubes such as thermos flasks and light bulbs.

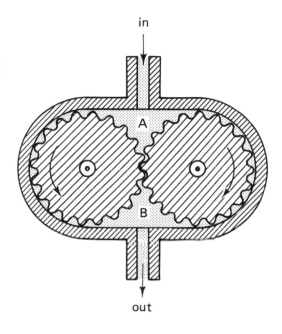

(b) Gear pump

The gear pump illustrated in (b) is used for pumping oil under high pressure for hydraulic rams on machines such as tractors and excavators. As the two gears mesh together they carry oil in the gaps between the gear teeth and the outer casing from A to B thus reducing the pressure in A and increasing it in B.

If A and B are connected to each end of a cylinder containing a piston, the effect is to push the piston along the cylinder. Reversing the direction of the gear wheels, pumps oil from B to A and hence pushes the piston in the opposite direction.

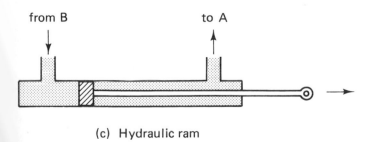

(c) Hydraulic ram

Air blowers are usually designed to pump a large volume of air and there have been some ingenious solutions to this problem. The two illustrated in (d) both involve two rotors which always remain in contact with each other as they rotate at the same speed in opposite directions. It is fascinating to see what different shapes have this property. Simple cylindrical rollers clearly do, as do a pair of gear wheels, but the shapes above come as something of a surprise. See if you can find other solutions.

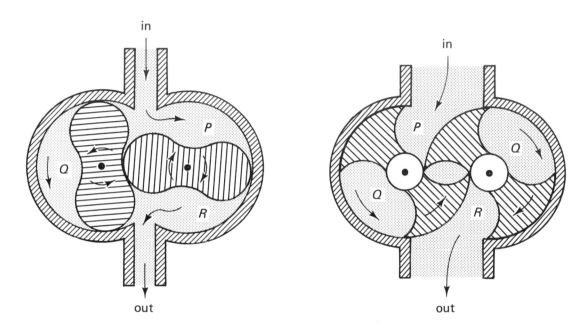

(d) Air blowers

creating spaces with changing volumes which draw in the oil at one part of the cycle and discharge it at another, see figure (e). This pump is known as a lobe pump and has one rotor turning inside another. The outer rotor has five symmetrically placed lobes while the inner rotor has four lobes which engage in the outer rotor and turn it. Because of the different number of lobes and the fact that the rotors turn about different axes (in the diagram the centre of the inner rotor is below that of the outer rotor) the spaces between the two rotors change in shape, although the total volume

In these blowers air is sucked into the space P, trapped inside space Q, and ejected at R as the space closes up.

The typical design for the oil-pump for the engine of a car is different again but the essential feature is retained of rotors

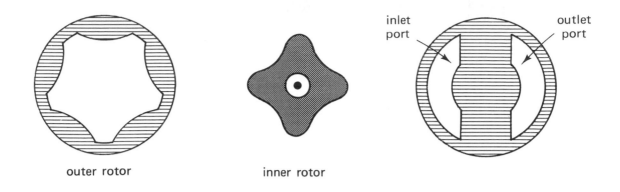

outer rotor   inner rotor

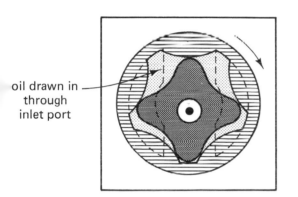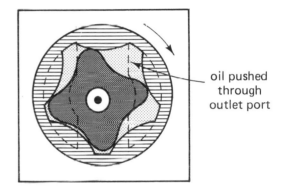

oil drawn in through inlet port

oil pushed through outlet port

(e) Lobe type oil-pump

between them is necessarily constant. The design of the rotors is such that the space opens up between them when they are above the inlet port, and reduces when they are above the outlet port.

The foregoing designs are all good examples of kinematics; this is the branch of mathematics that concerns itself with the geometrical aspects of objects in motion. It is an essential ingredient of the training for a good engineer. The study of mechanisms is closely linked with kinematics and can be used to give meaning to the teaching of motion geometry in schools.

63 Calendar capers

Because the numbers on a calendar occur in 7
columns there is a regularity about their pattern
which can be exploited in some simple tricks.

Ask someone to add together three numbers which
come immediately beneath each other in a column
and give the total. Suppose the total came to 45 then
you can very quickly give them the three dates they
have added, for the middle date is ⅓ of the total (i.e.
15) and the other dates are 7 each side of it (i.e. 8 and
22).

What were the dates when the total given was 57?

How could you adapt the method if someone gave
you the total for five numbers in a column?

One of the columns of five numbers above totals
85. Which one? You should have no need to add up
any of the columns.

When you start looking at the pages of calendars,
no matter for which month or year, you will realise
that the same numbers always occur underneath one
another for they step up in 7s, so, for example, 18 is
always below 11 and 25 always below 18.

Why can't a column which starts with 6 have five
numbers in it?

Can you devise a method to give the dates when
you are told the total of four numbers which came
underneath each other?

Relationships can easily be established between the dates
inside a 2 × 2 square or 3 × 3 square and their totals.

With a 2 × 2 square for example the total is always

$$4 \times (\text{smallest date} + 4)$$

and this can be used both ways:

(a) ask someone to give you the total and then you give the
dates

or

(b) ask someone to give you the smallest number and then
you give them the total.

Why does it work?

Suppose the smallest date is D then the four dates are

D	$D+1$
$D+7$	$D+8$

with a total of $T = 4D + 16$ which is equal to $4(D+4)$.

Suppose you were given the total T then to find D first
divide by 4 to find $D + 4$ then subtract 4.

Sun	Mon	Tue	Wed	Thu	Fri	Sat
				1	2	3
4	5	6	7	8	9	10
11	12	13	14	15	16	17
18	19	20	21	22	23	24
25	26	27	28	29	30	31

Sun	Mon	Tue	Wed	Thu	Fri	Sat
	1	2	3	4	5	6
7	8	9	10	11	12	13
14	15	16	17	18	19	20
21	22	23	24	25	26	27
28	29	30	31			

$$T \rightarrow \boxed{\div 4} \Rrightarrow \boxed{-4} \rightarrow D$$

The other three dates are then easily found by adding 1 to give $D + 1$, adding another 6 to give $D + 7$, and another 1 to give $D + 8$.

So, for example, if $T = 44$, then $D = \frac{44}{4} - 4 = 7$ and the other dates are 8, 14 and 15.

Now consider a 3×3 block. Here the pattern of numbers can be seen as

$C - 8$	$C - 7$	$C - 6$
$C - 1$	C	$C + 1$
$C + 6$	$C + 7$	$C + 8$

whose total will be $9C$ where C is the centre number.

Thus if you are presented with the total for a square block of nine numbers you have only to divide by 9 to find the centre number. It is then an easy matter to move up and down 7 to give the other numbers in the centre column, and up and down 1 from these numbers to give the numbers in the other columns.

For example, given the total as 108 quickly find

$$C = 108 \div 9 = 12.$$

Complete the centre column by

$$12 - 7 = 5 \text{ and } 12 + 7 = 19.$$

Find the left-hand column by subtracting 1 from each:

4,   11,   18.

Find the right-hand column by adding 1 to each:

6,   13,   20.

Alternatively, suppose someone told you that the largest number in a 3×3 square was 23 and challenged you to find the total of the dates in the square. As long as you remember the underlying pattern you would know that $23 = C + 8$ so $C = 15$ from which the total is $9C = 135$.

Devise methods for giving the dates when you are told the total of the dates forming a cross shape or an H shape as shown above … or try a shape of your own.

In a 2×2 square why is it that the product of the numbers on one diagonal is always 7 more than the product of the numbers on the other diagonal?

Investigate the sum of the numbers in a 3×3 square along the two diagonals and along the middle column and middle row.

Can such a square ever be magic?

Sun	Mon	Tue	Wed	Thu	Fri	Sat
		1	2	3	4	5
6	7	8	9	10	11	12
13	14	15	16	17	18	19
20	21	22	23	24	25	26
27	28	29	30	31		

64 The travelling salesman problem

There are many times when people have to visit a number of different places and then return to the starting point. They will often want to find the shortest possible route. Such a situation is called *the travelling salesman problem*, for it is one which salesmen face on most days of their working lives.

It is, however, a problem which many people would like to solve: for example,
— the oil-tanker driver who has to take petrol to a number of different filling stations,
— the driver of a milk-tanker who has to visit scattered farms,
— the American tourist who wants to visit Cambridge, Stratford-on-Avon, Edinburgh, Plymouth and Stonehenge.

Consider Mrs Lavender, a saleswoman based in Exeter, who has to visit the local towns shown on the map (a) to sell cosmetics. The numbers on the roads give the distance in miles between the towns. What is the shortest route she can take which will both start and end at Exeter?

(a)

Tiverton
Crediton
Cullompton
11
14
8
16
8
13
EXETER
16
23
10
24
Okehampton
Exmouth

(b)

Tiverton
Crediton
Cullompt
11
8
8
EXETER
23
23
24
Okehampton
10
Exmout

One popular method used to solve this type of problem is the *nearest city* approach. This means that Mrs Lavender will begin by going to the nearest town to Exeter. This is Crediton. Next she goes to the nearest town to Crediton she has not already visited and so on. This leads to the solution shown in (b). First we have the loop Exeter, Crediton, Tiverton, Cullompton, Exmouth and back to Exeter. After that there is the short loop Exeter, Okehampton, Exeter.

The total distance following this route is 107 miles, which is not the shortest. In practice it may use better roads and be the quickest, but we are only looking for the shortest distance.

A solution which you may have discovered for yourself is shown in (c). The basic idea behind this solution is to put all the towns on a single loop. This gives us an answer of 92 miles. This is much better than the previous one. It is still not the best solution, however. There is a route which is only 91 miles long. Can you find it?

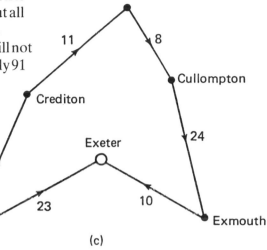

(c)

Suppose Mrs Lavender adds Honiton to the list of towns she will visit. What will now be the shortest route visiting all the towns (starting and ending at Exeter)? Could Mrs Lavender find a shorter route if she started and finished at Cullompton?

Does it make any difference which town you start and finish at?

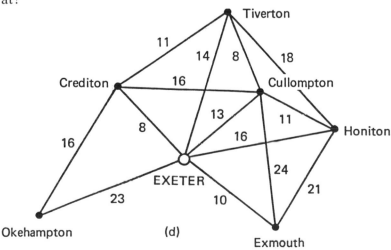

(d)

69

If Mrs Lavender did not have to finish at the town where she started, which towns should she start and end at to give the shortest route?

Mathematicians have tried hard to find ways of solving problems like these. So far they have been unsuccessful. They know that a shortest route cannot cross itself. However, the methods they know for finding exact solutions are no use for complicated problems with many towns. They take too long to run even on a large modern computer! There are ways of finding 'good' solutions (which might not be the best) which use organised 'trial and error', but anyone who can find a straightforward and fast way to get the best route will make a fortune!

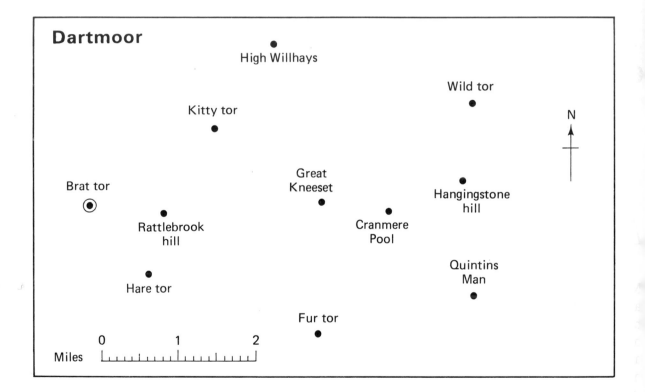

Dartmoor

Every year thousands of teenagers take part in the Ten Tors expedition which involves walking over Dartmoor and visiting tors (granite outcrops usually found on hilltops) such as those given on the map below. For months in advance of the actual event teams can be found training on the moor every weekend. One weekend a team set out from Brat Tor on a map-reading exercise with the object of visiting all the places named on the map shown and returning to their starting point. Find the shortest route they could take.

One way to approach the solution of this type of problem is to make a tracing of the map and pin it to a drawing board.

Then stick pins in at each of the places to be visited and use lengths of different coloured cotton to mark out possible routes. The shortest piece would of course correspond to the best route.

Investigate problems of this kind in your own locality using an Ordnance Survey map or an AA book.

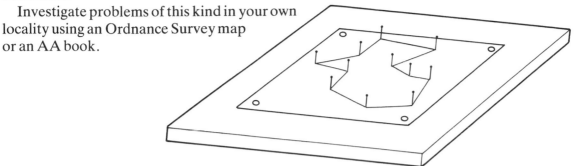

65 The volume of a hemisphere

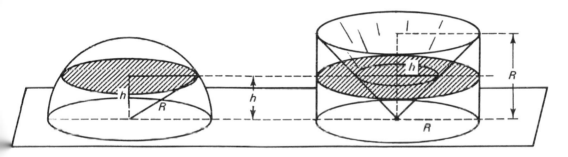

Many of you will know the formula for the volume of a sphere and hence the volume of a hemisphere, but not many will have met the fascinating relation between the volumes of a hemisphere of radius R, a cylinder of radius and height R, and a cone of radius and height R. The volume of the hemisphere is in fact the volume between the cylinder and the cone, and this can be demonstrated neatly by showing that the area of cross-section of each at a height h from the base is always the same; see the shaded areas in the diagram. The shaded cross-section of the hemisphere is a circle of radius $\surd(R^2 - h^2)$ so its area is $\pi(R^2 - h^2)$. Now the shaded area between the cylinder and the cone is a circular annulus with outer and inner radii of R and h respectively. (The inner radius is h because the semi-vertical angle of the cone is $45°$.) So the area of the annulus is also $\pi(R^2 - h^2)$.

This relationship was known to Chinese mathematicians a long time ago and may well have led to a formula for the volume of a sphere.

66 Transformation treasure trove

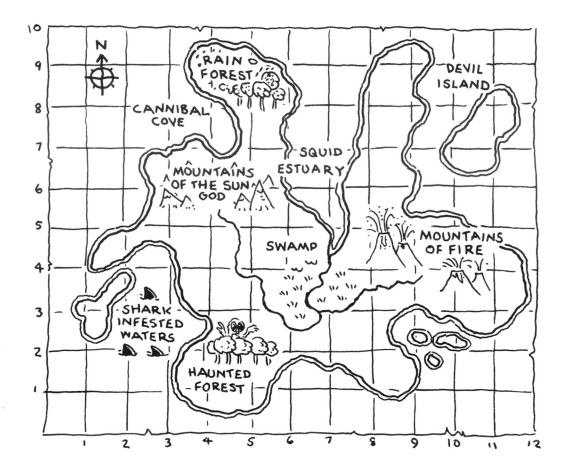

A modern pirate hid his treasure of gold bullion worth millions of dollars on a small island in the Caribbean. So that he could locate his gold at a later date he drew a map of the island on a square grid (see the copy of it above) and made up a series of clues. His clues were in the form of a sequence of transformations which he knew would baffle his crew of desperadoes but shouldn't cause you too many problems if you start with a piece of squared paper and follow the instructions carefully.

1 Land on the small off-shore island at $(1, 3)$.

2 Travel East $\begin{pmatrix} 3 \\ 0 \end{pmatrix}$ to the main island.

3 Reflect in $y = 5$ and beware of head hunters!

4 Reflect in $x = 5$ but don't swim off this coast!

5 Rotate through 180° about $(7, 6)$ and keep cool!

6 Reflect in $y = x$ and don't forget your oilskins!

7 Translate $\begin{pmatrix} 6 \\ -1 \end{pmatrix}$ and say your prayers!

8 Rotate through 90° clockwise about $(7, 7)$ to find the treasure under a large boulder.

67 The variable menu

The owner of a transport cafe had many regular customers. So as not to bore them with a monotonous menu she devised a plan which would ensure that no two meals should repeat themselves for at least a year. She saw each meal as basically consisting of 4 parts (i) potatoes or equivalent, (ii) meat or fish (iii) a vegetable, (iv) a sweet. Her solution is embodied in the following table.

chips	pork	peas	apple pie
boiled potatoes	lamb	carrots	ice cream
roast potatoes	chicken	sweet corn	fruit salad
rice	fish	cabbage	
	beef	cauliflower	
		brussels sprouts	
		broad beans	

Starting on the first day of the year she served chips, pork, peas and apple pie and on each succeeding day she replaced each part of the meal by the next ingredient in the table. The next ingredient to the one at the bottom of a column being the one at the top so, for example, if on one day the meal was rice, fish, broad beans, and apple pie, on the next day it would be chips, beef, peas, and ice cream.

How many days pass before a meal repeats itself?

What meal is served on day 100 from the start of the scheme?

On what day would you expect to be served roast potatoes, lamb, brussels sprouts and apple pie?

The cafe became known for its variable menu and the trade increased so much that the owner appointed a new cook. Thinking to please the owner the new cook extended the table above by adding sausages to the meat column and turnips to the vegetable column. Why did the owner sack him?

68 Loop-line limitations

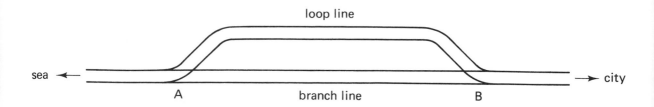

loop line

sea ← → city

A   branch line   B

The branch line from the city main line station to a popular
seaside resort only justified a single line because for most of
the year the passenger traffic was light. This did create
problems in the busy holiday period however so the railway
company added a short loop line at the half-way point to
allow trains to pass one another and thus enable trains to
travel along the line in both directions at the same time. The
loop line and the branch line between the points at A and B,
see the diagram, could each take an engine and six carriages,
or seven carriages.

   This made passing easy as long as one of two trains meeting
at this point could be wholly contained by the loop.
Unfortunately on a busy Bank Holiday a relief station master
allowed a train with 14 carriages to leave the seaside just as a
train with 16 carriages left the city headed towards the sea.
Many cross words were exchanged by the engine drivers
when they met at the half-way point, but before they came to
blows one of the passengers showed them an efficient way out
of their dilemma. The passenger was a life-long puzzle freak
and she saw the situation as an occasion to put her problem
solving skills to practical use. She convinced the drivers that
they could pass each other with a minimum of fuss – indeed
one of the trains could stay coupled together for the whole of
the operation. Show how the trains can pass with the
minimum of stopping and starting by the engines.

69 Which was the winning strategy?

In a cross-country race four friends each decided on a different strategy towards the way they ran.

Alan decided to run half the distance at 16 km/h and half the distance at 8 km/h.

Bruce ran at 16 km/h for half the time and jogged at 8 km/h for the remaining time.

Christine decided to run at a steady pace of 12 km/h throughout.

Daphne counted her paces as she ran and reckoned to run half of her paces at 16 km/h and the other half at 8 km/h. In what order did they finish?

70 A topological trick

At a party Norman and Nuala were tied together as shown and challenged to separate themselves without untying the string or cutting it. To make it quite clear, Norman has one end of a piece of string tied around his right wrist, A, and the other end tied around his left wrist, B. Nuala has a second piece of string with one end tied around her left wrist, and then looped under and over Norman's string before the other end is tied around her right wrist, Q. Try it yourself with a friend. It may look impossible to solve at first but there is a neat way of unravelling yourselves which doesn't require any acrobatics.

71 Parallel constraints

It is easy to construct an equilateral triangle such as *ABC* and then to draw three parallel lines *l*, *m* and *n* through its vertices as shown in the diagram.

However, if you start by drawing three parallel lines and then set yourself the task of constructing an equilateral triangle with one vertex on each line you will have to start thinking.

You could take any point on one of the lines to begin with as a vertex of the proposed triangle, but what size is the triangle, and how is it to be orientated?

A similar problem is to construct a square with one vertex on each of the sides of a parallelogram, where the sides may be produced if required.

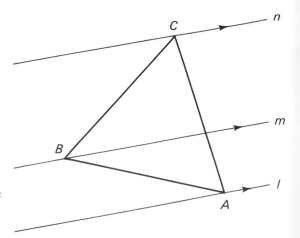

72 Hidden shapes

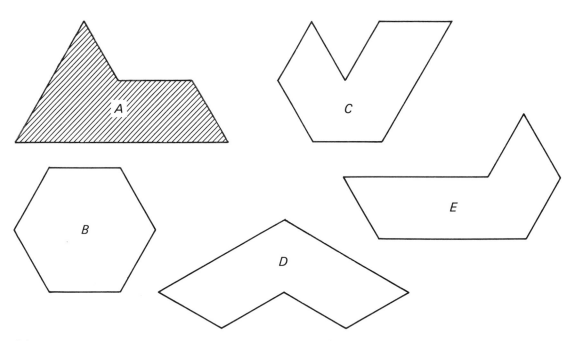

(*a*) The sphinx-like shape *A* can be cut into *two* identical pieces which can be rearranged to form many different shapes including *B*, *C*, *D* and *E*. See what different shapes you can find.

(*b*) Shape *A* has the further interesting property that it can be divided into *four* equal parts which are identical in shape to *A* itself. Can you find them?

What other shapes have this property?

(c) The trapezium shape T can also be obtained from A by dividing it into two pieces of equal area and rearranging them. How?

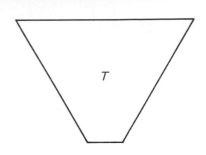

73 Sim

This is a simple game for two players devised by Gustavus Simmons (hence its name).

Play starts with the six points A, B, C, D, E, F at the vertices of a hexagon inscribed in a circle. Players, using different coloured pencils or pens take turns to join a pair of the vertices with a straight line.

There are fifteen possible lines so the game must finish in a limited time, and the aim of the game is to avoid making a triangle of your colour, with vertices on the circle. If you do, you lose. Interestingly, it is not possible to draw all fifteen lines with two colours and avoid a triangle of one colour, so someone must lose!

The result of one game is shown here, with numbers to indicate the order in which the lines were drawn. The solid lines represent the first player P and the dotted lines the second player Q. It is Q's turn and the only possible moves are DF which completes DAF, and FE which completes EAF. So Q must lose.

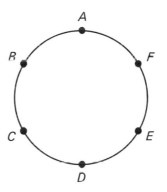

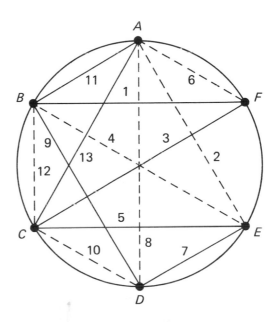

74 Boxes

Boxes is a game that most children play at some time while at school. First, a rectangular array of dots is marked on a piece of paper, then two people take turns to join an adjacent pair of dots to form the side of a square (box).

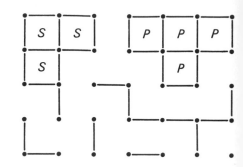

When players see three sides of a square already drawn then they can (in their turn) complete the square and claim it by writing in their initial. Further, when a player completes a square, that person has another turn. When all the boxes are drawn the person claiming the most squares wins.

This is an easy game to play, and for most children it is played without much thought, but a little analysis would not go amiss. Overall strategies are not easy but the recognition of the possibilities in certain patterns of lines can be discussed and should influence play.

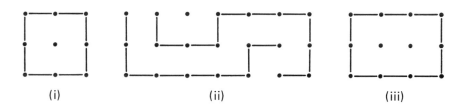

(i)   (ii)   (iii)

The player who first adds a line inside the 2×2 square shown in (i) immediately loses all the four squares inside it to their opponent. A channel one square wide, no matter how it twists or turns, is highly vulnerable, see (ii). The first person to add a line inside it will be allowing the next player to claim the squares throughout its length.

The 3×2 rectangle in (iii) is interesting. If it is the final region left and it is your turn, if you draw a line in from the side of the rectangle you will give two squares to your opponent who will then have to add a line which will give you the remaining four squares. However, if you draw in the line across the middle joining the isolated dots your opponent will be forced to give you all six squares.

Much can be learned by playing mini-games where a boundary is already drawn in and the outcomes quite limited, such as with the 4×2 rectangle shown.

(a) Suppose A plays first and draws the line from the middle of the left-hand edge and B replies by completing the two squares presenting themselves and then draws the bar in the middle of them. Whatever A does now B will be able to claim all the squares.

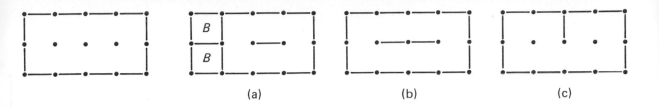

(a)　　　　　　　　　(b)　　　　　　　　　(c)

(*b*) Suppose *A* draws in one of the bars joining two of the isolated dots then *B*, if wide awake, will play the adjoining central bar, so that any move by *A* will give all eight squares to *B*.

(*c*) The best that *A* can do is to gain half the squares in the rectangle. To do this *A* must first draw a line from the middle of one of the long sides. Follow this through and see that the outcome will be four squares each to *A* and *B* whatever *B* plays next.

When play has been analysed inside these smaller shapes then the strategy of play on a larger grid could be closely linked to sub-dividing it into shapes where the possible plays are already understood.

75 Measuring the gear of a bicycle

The early bicycles such as the velocipede designed by Pierre Michaux (1867) and the penny-farthing by James Starley (1870) had pedals attached to the front wheel just as with a child's tricycle today. Each turn of the pedals produced one turn of the front wheel which moved the bicycle forward a distance equal to the wheel's circumference. Thus the larger the wheel the further the cycle would go for one turn of the pedals. The result was that the gear of the early bicycles depended entirely on the size of the wheel, the larger the wheel the higher the gear. Because of this the gear of a bicycle was defined as the diameter of the driving wheel measured in inches. So a penny-farthing would have something like a 50-inch gear whereas a child's tricycle would have something like a 10-inch gear.

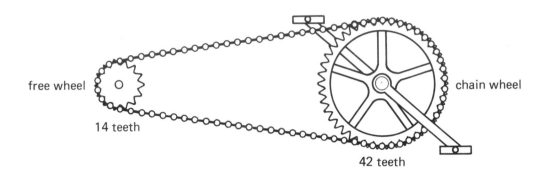

free wheel

14 teeth

chain wheel

42 teeth

   To this day the same essential idea is used for measuring the gear of a bicycle whether it has one gear or ten. Consider a bicycle with 27-inch wheels which has only one gear. The chain wheel has 42 teeth and drives the free wheel with 14 teeth. With this arrangement the free wheel will turn around three times for each turn of the pedals.
   The result is that for each turn of the pedals the rear wheel makes three revolutions so the cycle will travel as far as it would if it were a penny-farthing with a wheel of diameter $3 \times 27 = 81$ inches. (This is because the perimeter of a wheel is of course proportional to its diameter.) Because of this the cycle is said to have an 81-inch gear. This is larger than any ever achieved on a penny-farthing, where the maximum size of the large driving wheel was determined by the rider's inner leg measurement.
   See if you can spot a penny-farthing in a museum and estimate the diameter of its driving wheel.
   Direct drive cycles had very low gears, but as soon as the chain drive was introduced by Starley, on his Rover Safety Bicycle in 1885, cycle designs became very similar to those of today. By using a chain wheel attached to the pedals, with more teeth on it than the free wheel attached to the driving wheel, high gears can be obtained with relatively small driving wheels.

free wheel   chain wheel

Consider a typical BMX bicycle with 20-inch wheels, a chain wheel with 36 teeth and a free wheel with 18 teeth. As 36 is twice 18, the driving wheel will turn twice for every turn of the pedals so it has a 40-inch gear (i.e. twice the diameter of the driving wheel).

This is a relatively low gear, for BMX cycles are designed for stunting and acceleration not all-out speed. Contrast this with the 275-inch gear used by José Meiffret when he achieved the world speed record for a bicycle of just over 127 mph. You can see from the picture he was not riding a penny-farthing with a 23-foot diameter wheel! His bicycle had a driving wheel of 27.5 inch diameter and a chain wheel which had 10 times as many teeth as the free wheel.

To find the gear of a bicycle with a chain drive simply use the relation

$$\text{gear} = \frac{\text{No of teeth on chain wheel}}{\text{No of teeth on free wheel}} \times \text{diameter of driving wheel}$$

Many modern cycles have as many as ten gears to suit all possible conditions of wind and hills. This is achieved by having two different sized chain wheels and a free wheel made up of five different sized wheels side by side. The cycle shown here has chain wheels with 50 teeth and 32 teeth and a free wheel with 14, 17, 20, 24 and 28 teeth.

One mechanism can move the chain sideways to engage one of the chain wheels with any one of the sprockets on the free wheel. Another mechanism can move the chain from one chain wheel to the other. The lowest gear will be when the 32-tooth chain wheel drives the 28-tooth free wheel. Thus if the driving wheel has a 27-inch diameter

$$\text{lowest gear} = \frac{32}{28} \times 27 = 30.9 \text{ inch},$$

$$\text{highest gear} = \frac{50}{14} \times 27 = 96.4 \text{ inch}.$$

Copy and complete the following table to see what gears are available on this cycle.

		Number of teeth on free wheel				
		14	17	20	24	28
Number of teeth on chain wheel	32					30.9
	50	96.4				

The above data came from the Claude Butler specification for their women's Ladydale model but their men's Cresta 531 model specifies chain wheels with 40 teeth and 50 teeth along with the same free wheel.

If you were riding the Ladydale cycle and, starting in the lowest gear you worked your way up through the gears to the highest gear, how many times would you need to change the chain from one chain wheel to the other? Would you obtain the same answer using the Cresta 531 model?

The nice thing about defining cycle gears in this way is that it makes comparison between the gears of cycles of different wheel size and different types of gear relatively easy. This is even more significant now that cycle designs show such a variety of wheel size compared with the standard 26-inch or 27-inch wheel of a few years ago.

Investigate the gear sizes used by racing cyclists and compare them with the gear sizes of the small cycles often used about town and children's very first bicycles.

Hub type	Description	Hub ratios			
		First	Second	Third	Fourth
AW	3-speed wide ratio	.75	1	1.333	—
AM	3-speed medium ratio	.865	1	1.155	—
FW	4-speed wide ratio	.666	.79	1	1.266
FM	4-speed medium ratio	.666	.857	1	1.125
FC	4-speed close ratio	.9	1	1.091	—

Sturmey-Archer hub gear data

So far hub gears have not been discussed, but with the data given in the above table about Sturmey-Archer gears this can now be done.

What does this table mean?

The effect of the hub gear is to change the rate at which the driving wheel turns relative to the free wheel. Consider the 3-speed wide ratio hub gear (AW). In first gear (the lowest gear) the driving wheel only turns through 0.75 of a revolution for one revolution of the free wheel. In second gear the driving wheel turns through one revolution for one revolution of the free wheel, i.e. there is direct drive. In third gear the driving wheel turns through 1.333 revolutions for each turn of the free wheel.

83

Suppose now a bicycle with 26-inch wheels and fitted with the AW hub has a chain wheel with 46 teeth and a free wheel with 18 teeth, then

first gear $= \frac{46}{18} \times 26 \times 0.75 = 49.8$ inch

second gear $= \frac{46}{18} \times 26 \times 1 = 66.4$ inch

third gear $= \frac{46}{18} \times 26 \times 1.333 = 88.6$ inch

In general then

$$\text{gear} = \frac{\text{no of teeth on chain wheel}}{\text{no of teeth on free wheel}} \times \text{diameter of driving wheel} \times \text{hub ratio}$$

Use this to find the gears which the above bicycle would have if it was fitted with the other hubs given in the table.

Investigate the number of teeth for the four sprockets on a free wheel which would give gear ratios approximating to an FW hub.

By using two chain wheels, a free wheel with five sprockets and a hub gear a bicycle could have a very large number of gears. Investigate!

76   Three-dimensional doodles

How do you see the top drawing opposite? Try to imagine it as a piece of wire which starts at a, travels up away from Z, then towards X, then Y, then X, then away from Z, away from X ... etc. until it ends at b. This wire construction which looks like a piece of modern sculpture has been drawn by using three vanishing points, namely X, Y and Z and then drawing all the lines to or from one of them. Try to visualise what is happening in space to your imaginary piece of wire as you *bend* it into shape so that when it passes behind a piece of wire you leave a gap in the line drawn at that point.

This is a very useful convention to use in 3D drawings and makes them easier to understand. The feint lines are construction lines which can be carefully erased at the end. Start with simple designs and see what you can achieve.

The construction in (a) and (b) can be seen as formed from a continuous loop of wire. Make tracings of the drawings and find where the vanishing points are.

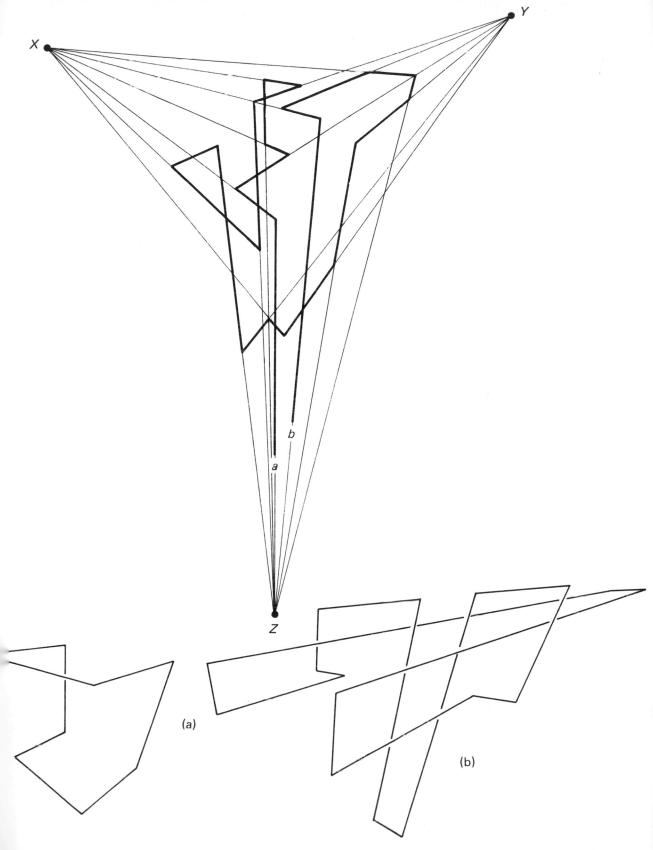

(a)

(b)

77 Palindromic termini

38 added to 83 gives 121 which is palindromic as the digits read the same from left to right as from right to left. What other 2-digit numbers have this property?

Starting with 68 and adding 86 gives 154 which is not palindromic, but if the process is repeated by reversing the digits of the sum and adding it to itself the result will eventually be palindromic:

$$68 + 86 = 154 \quad \text{not palindromic}$$
$$154 + 451 = 605 \quad \text{not palindromic}$$
$$605 + 506 = 1111 \quad \text{palindromic}$$

The number of steps required may be small or large: 89 for example, requires 24 steps before the sum becomes palindromic. No one has yet determined whether this will happen when 196 is taken as the starting point.

Investigate what happens when starting with other numbers – you need not restrict yourself to 2-digit numbers as a starting point.

78 About turn!

It is not too difficult to find numbers such that

$$abc \times def = ghijk$$
$$\text{and} \quad cba \times fed = kjihg$$

are both true at the same time, for example

$$131 \times 111 = 14541$$
$$\text{and} \quad 102 \times 201 = 20502$$

which rely on symmetry. However solutions can be found where no symmetry exists, for example

$$312 \times 221 = 68952$$

when turned about gives

$$213 \times 122 = 25986$$

which is also true.

How many other solutions can you find?

Try to find the relationships between the digits a, b, c and d, e, f, for the products to be reversible.

79 Round and around

Look at the very special pattern in these divisions

$$4\overline{)615\,384}$$
$$153\,846$$

$$4\overline{)410\,256}$$
$$102\,564$$

The quotient appears to be obtained by moving the left-hand digit to the right-hand end of the number being divided by 4.

$$615\,384 \div 4 = \textcircled{6}\,153\,84$$
$$419\,256 \div 4 = \textcircled{4}\,102\,56$$

Check that the same pattern is also true when 102 564 is divided by 4.

The question arises, 'Are these numbers unique?'. You can soon prove to yourself that they are not, by completing the following so that the same pattern holds

$$4\overline{)92****}$$
$$23****$$

$$4\overline{)3*****}$$
$$*****3$$

Notice how in both these cases the order of the digits is the same when they are thought of as continuous cycles.

Now complete the following in the same way

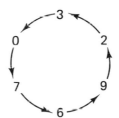

$$4\overline{)8*****}$$
$$*****8$$

$$4\overline{)5*****}$$
$$*****5$$

$$4\overline{)2*****}$$
$$*****2$$

So far only division by 4 has been considered. Can similar patterns be found when dividing by other numbers? Consider division by 2 for example:

$$2\overline{)315\,789\,473\,684\,210\,526}$$
$$157\,894\,736\,842\,105\,263$$

This time a cycle of 18 digits was needed before the required pattern could be achieved.

Try completing the following:

$$2\overline{)5}$$
$$2\overline{)7}$$
$$2\overline{)9}$$

What do you notice?

Investigate the length of the cycle needed to achieve the pattern when dividing by 3.

Can you explain the results?

80 Insights into the icosahedron

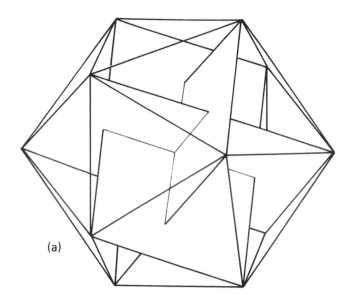

(a)

When a pair of opposite edges of an icosahedron are joined they form a rectangle whose sides are in the ratio of the golden section (approximately 1.618). If three such identical rectangles are cut out of card and slotted together symmetrically as shown above then their twelve vertices lie at the vertices of a regular icosahedron.

To make an icosahedron in this way use thick card and rectangles of say 13 cm by 8 cm (consecutive numbers in a Fibonacci sequence make a good approximation to the golden section ratio; see for example *Mathematical Activities* p. 127). Cut slits in the cards to slot them together and then use coloured wool or shirring elastic to complete the edges. A small notch at each corner will help to fix these edges securely.

The American genius Buckminster Fuller made a particular study of structures consisting of struts and tensioning wires and is famous for his designs of geodesic domes. Much of this study was concerned with minimum structures for keeping a given number of points fixed in place in space and the drawing (b) shows his solution for the twelve vertices of a regular icosahedron. It consists of six equal struts in compression, which lie in the positions represented by the long edges of the card rectangles in the earlier model, together with wire or nylon thread connecting their ends, in tension.

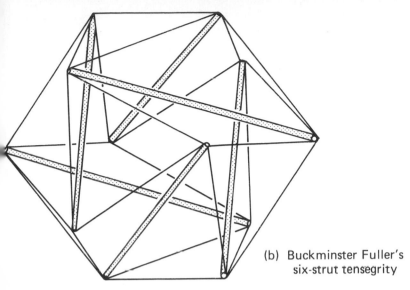

(b) Buckminster Fuller's
six-strut tensegrity

The drawing may appear to have some lines missing, for Buckminster Fuller discovered he did not need wires corresponding to all the edges of the icosahedron to keep his struts rigid. If you look carefully you will see four wires connecting the top of each strut in contrast to the five edges of a complete icosahedron at each vertex – but this makes the model all the more fascinating.

The model is not as difficult to make as it might first appear. Start by getting some 6 mm dowel rod and cutting from it six struts each 30 cm long. Next with a saw make a narrow cut 5 mm deep into the end of each strut. The struts are then joined together using six loops of string or nylon cord. The length of cord in each loop is critical, and with the struts here each loop such as $ABCD$ and $PQRS$ in the diagram should be 72 cm long when in tension. To achieve this make your loops by tying them tightly around a piece of card or hardboard which is 36 cm wide.

It is important for ease of construction of the model that the cord used fits tightly in the saw cuts at the ends of the struts so that they stay in place when not under tension.

First fit four struts and two loops together as shown above and then use the four remaining loops to add in the last two struts.

This is a very satisfying model to build and display.

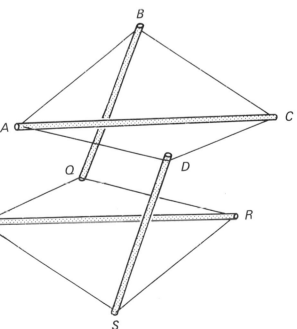

81   Factors galore

The number 3 785 942 160 made up of the ten digits 0, 1, 2, ...,
9 is divisible by all the integers from 1 to 18 inclusive. How
many other such numbers can you find?

82   Fascinating fractions

The digits 1, 2, 3, ..., 9 can be arranged to form two numbers
whose ratio is ½ as follows

$$\frac{7329}{14\,658} = \frac{1}{2}$$

This is interesting in itself, but even more fascinating is the
fact that the nine digits can also be arranged to form numbers
whose ratio is ⅓, ¼, ⅕, ⅙, ⅐, ⅛, ⅑.

   Get your calculator to work and see how many solutions
you can find.

83   How large a number can you make

You can use the digits 1, 2 and 3 once only and any
mathematical symbols you are aware of, but no symbol is to
be used more than once. The challenge is to see who can
make the largest number. Here are some numbers to set the
ball rolling.

   321   21^3 $(3 \div .1)^2$

84 Surakarta

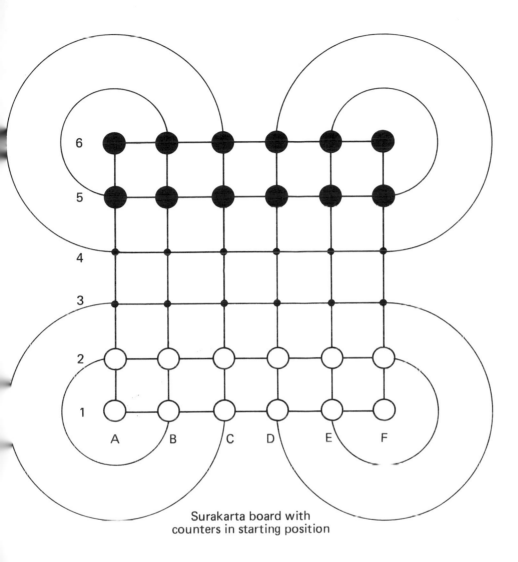

Surakarta board with
counters in starting position

urakarta is an Indonesian game for two players named after
he town in Java where it originated and it deserves to be
etter known. The board consists of a network of squares
ith interconnecting arcs of circles at the corners as shown
bove. Each player has 12 counters of a distinguishable
olour and they are set out facing each other in two ranks of 6
t the start of the game. The players draw lots or spin a coin to
ee who starts, then take turns moving one piece at a time.
   A move consists of moving a counter along a line *or*
iagonally to an adjacent vacant point so, for example, at the
art the piece on C2 can move to B3 or C3 or D3.
   The object of the game is to capture one's opponent's
eces, and this is where the circular arcs come into play. A

piece can only capture another piece when it has a clear path
along the lines on the board, which must include a circular arc
(or arcs) to that piece. When this is the case a piece can travel
any distance along this path and ends up in the position of the
opponent's piece which is removed from the board.
Diagrams (a) and (b) show several examples of capture.

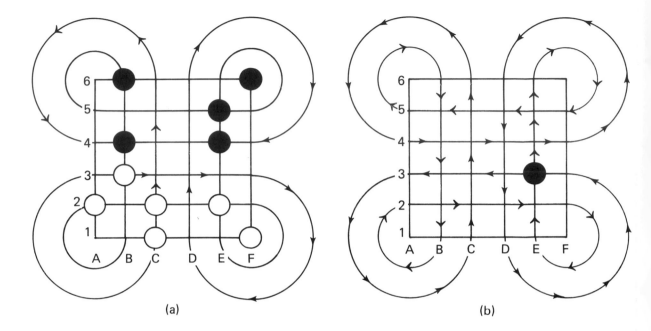

(a)   (b)

    In (a) the white counter on C2 can travel up to C6, around
the circle and along line 4 to capture the black counter on B4.
The white counter on B3, although adjacent to the black
counter on B4 cannot capture it as all routes between them
which involve circles are blocked by other pieces.

    However, the counter on B3 can move to the right along
line 3, around the circular arc, up line D, around a second
circular arc to capture the black counter on E4.

    Note that all paths are two-way so that if white is in a
position to capture black then black would also be able to
capture white.

    The circular paths, which can only be traversed when
capturing an opponent's piece, are a unique feature of this
game and give it a special interest.

    Figure (b) illustrates the powerful attacking position of a
point such as E3. By travelling up or down initially the path
connects all the smaller circles, while by moving sideways
initially all the lines connecting the large circles are accessible
– always supposing there is no piece in the way. The potential
of such a position to capturing opponent's pawns however is
also its vulnerability to being attacked. The only positions on

the board which are free from attack are the points at the
centres of the circles.

The winner is the player who first reduces his opponent's
'army' to an agreed number, *or* the player with the largest
'army' on the board when time is called.

Draw yourself a board on a piece of card and try it out. You
will need eyes like a hawk to watch those attacks coming from
all sides!

For a more permanent board mark out the network on a
piece of plywood and drill holes at the points to take coloured
pegs.

85 Catch your shadow

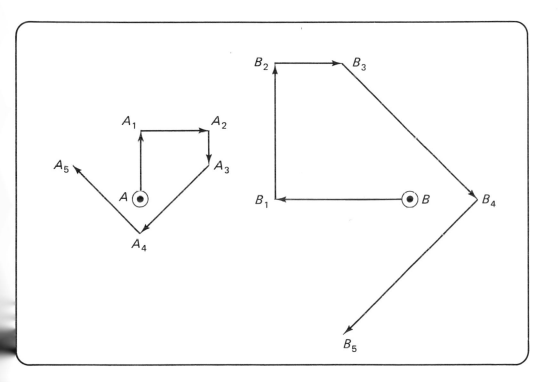

Starting at *A* a person can trace out a route on the visual
display unit of a computer. The computer has been
programmed to start at *B* and produce an image of *A*'s trace
having transformed it in a systematic way. The challenge is
for the person operating the computer to decide what
transformation is taking place and then to construct a route
so that *A* and *B* coincide. One person's attempt is shown on
the screen above and should be more than sufficient for you
to see what transformation is taking place, but can you catch
your shadow?

86 Number pyramids

In the number pyramids which follow the numbers in each new level of the pyramid are derived from the level below by the simple addition rule shown on the right. Find the missing numbers in each case.

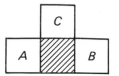

$C = A + B$

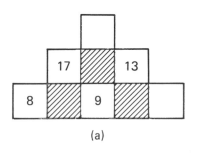

(a)

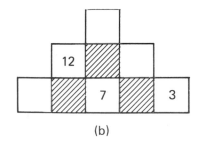

(b)

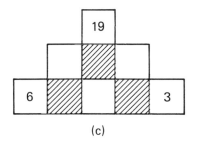

(c)

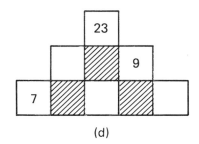

(d)

87   Can you help the block manufacturer?

A manufacturer was keen to design a new size of concrete block with the property that if it was cut in half through the plane of symmetry which bisected its long edges then the resulting halves would have exactly the same shape as the original block.

He wanted the shortest edge of the block to be 10 cm. What lengths should he make the other edges?

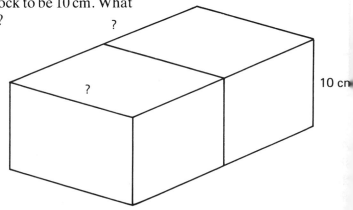

88 The Old Girls' reunion

At their school's annual reunion five friends shared a table for dinner. Each friend ordered something to drink, a meat course and a dessert. Brenda and Mrs Burns had martinis while Betty and Mrs Brown ordered sherry. Ms Baker had a fruit juice since she was driving. Brenda and Miss Broad ordered steak. Beryl and Ms Baker had roast beef. For dessert Beryl and Miss Black ate gateau, while Barbara and Ms Baker had ice cream. The other friend had a fruit salad. No two friends sitting next to each other were served two things the same.

Who had duck and what did Bridget eat?

89 Amoeboid patterns

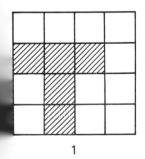

1

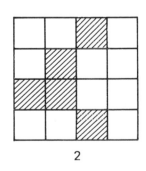

2

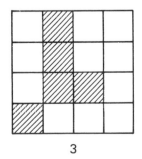

3

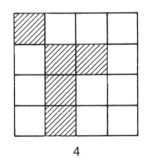

4

Amoebas move by changing their shape. The sequence of shapes above all have the same area and change from one to the next by a simple rule. Find the rule and give the next two shapes. Will the shape ever return to its original position?

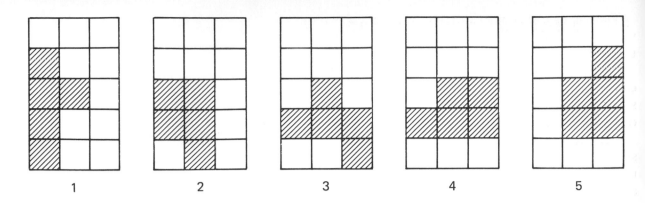

1   2   3   4   5

Spot the rule in this second amoeboid pattern and investigate the different shapes which are generated.

Try making up rules of your own to generate shapes.

90   Make squares

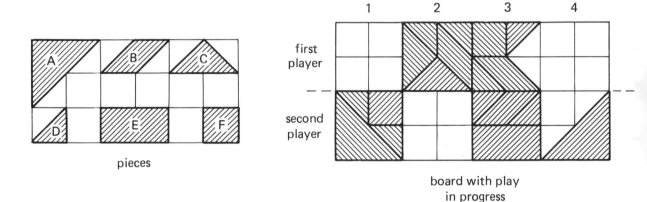

pieces

board with play
in progress

This is a board game for two players.

The playing pieces are cards shaped like A, B, C, D, E and F. For each player make a set of sixteen pieces as follows. On a 3 cm square grid draw then cut out: 2 of shape A, 3 of shape B, 3 of shape C, 6 of shape D, 1 of shape E and 1 of shape F. It is less confusing if the shapes for each player are of a different colour.

The playing surface consists of a board marked out with eight 2 × 2 squares (i.e. 6 cm by 6 cm) as shown above, with four squares for each player. Having decided who shall play first, players in turn add a piece to the board. When a piece has been placed on the board it cannot be moved, and the object is to complete as many squares as possible – no overlapping of pieces allowed.

The player who completes the largest number of squares wins. It is possible to complete all four squares but this is unlikely with beginners.

With experienced players the game can be made more challenging by insisting that the pieces are placed in the squares in the order 1, 2, 3, 4, 1, 2, 3, 4, etc. and not building one square after another.

Related to this game is the interesting investigation of seeing just what different ways a 2 × 2 square could be made up using pieces like A, B, …, F. This could form a group activity with results recorded on large squared paper for all to see … or a competition with a point for each different solution, or for a solution that no one else has. Beware of discussion/argument on mirror images and rotated solutions!

91   Measuring the bounce of a ball

Most people have watched or played a variety of ball games – tennis, hockey, football, squash, golf, cricket, basketball, snooker to name but a few. In all these games the bounce of the ball off the playing surfaces is very important and for this reason manufacturers have to make balls so that their bounce agrees with the standards set down by each game's organising body.

A tennis ball is made so that when it is dropped from a height of 200 cm onto a concrete surface, it should bounce to a height of between 106 cm and 116 cm. Get hold of some tennis balls and test them for yourself. It is all very well to know this about a tennis ball but does it tell us anything about how it would bounce if dropped from a different height, say 100 cm?

H (cm)	h (cm)
50	23
100	61
150	77
200	97
250	126
300	146

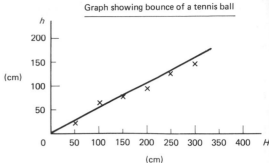

Graph showing bounce of a tennis ball

An experiment was carried out with a tennis ball by dropping it from different heights (H cm) onto a paving slab, and measuring the heights (h cm) to which the ball bounced. The results are summarised by the table and the graph. In this case the ball appears always to rise to approximately the same fraction of the height from which it was dropped,

$$\frac{h}{H} \simeq \frac{1}{2},$$

and the best fit for the experimental data is a straight line graph through the origin with gradient ½.

Most well-made balls show this consistency when dropped onto a relatively hard surface from a wide range of heights – golf balls are particularly good in this respect in contrast to table tennis balls which are affected by air resistance.

It is interesting to investigate the bounce of a tennis ball on different playing surfaces such as clay, grass, boards etc. for it will help one appreciate why some players are more successful on one surface than another. The Swedish tennis federation were well aware of this when they constructed especially *slow* clay courts for the Davis cup tie against the USA in 1985 and had an historic win.

How well does a tennis ball bounce off a racket? Investigate the difference with different kinds of stringing and different tensions as well as different parts of the face of the racket.

Knowing the ratio h/H for a given ball on a particular surface enables us to predict how high it will bounce on successive bounces, so for a golf ball dropped from 80 cm onto a classroom floor where this ratio is about ½ the successive bounce will have heights of about 40 cm, 20 cm, 10 cm etc. Try it and see for yourself.

Which do you think bounces the best, a golf ball, a basketball, a steel ball-bearing, a table tennis ball?

Well the answer will depend on the kind of surface on which the balls are bounced. If the surface was as hard as steel then the ball-bearing would do best, but if it were a softer surface then the ball-bearing would deform the surface and not bounce nearly as well as say a basketball.

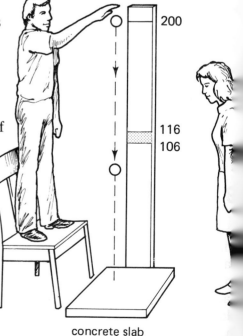

concrete slab

Footballers, cricketers, golfers and hockey players are well aware of the problems of bounce on different playing surfaces. The new Astro Turf used by some professional football teams has come in for much criticism by visiting teams who find it difficult to adjust to the higher bouncing ball.

From time to time manufacturers produce balls with more bounce in the hope of increasing their sales. An American firm produced a bouncier golf ball, but players were hitting it so far they reached the greens too easily and it was banned. Recently the Australian-made Merco squash ball proved to be too *lively* so that top tournament players found it difficult to play a winning shot and rallies went on for too long.

Temperature plays a significant role in the bouncing characteristics of hollow balls where the air pressure inside them increases with temperature. At Wimbledon the new tennis balls are kept in a temperature controlled chest before being used because of this fact. A cold squash ball is almost unplayable because of its lack of bounce.

There is more scope for practical work here. Try heating a table tennis ball to different temperatures by using a fridge and a kettle of water and investigating the height to which it bounces when released at a height of one metre onto a hard surface.

92 Seeing is believing

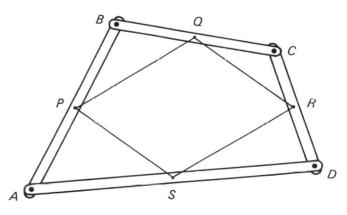

Make up a quadrilateral *ABCD* from card strips and paper fasteners. Now join the mid-points of the strips to each other using shirring elastic or elastic bands as in the diagram. No matter how you change the shape of the quadrilateral, the mid-points *PQRS* always form a parallelogram.

93 Band constructions

Using your ruler draw two sets of equally spaced parallel lines as shown, where the distances between the lines is equal to the width of your ruler. The result is a tessellation of parallelograms. By varying the angles between your two sets of lines you will obtain parallelograms of different shapes but they are still very special. Hold this page so that the long diagonals of the parallelograms go up and down and you will see they are in fact diamond shaped or what a mathematician calls a rhombus. What shape would they be if your two sets of parallels had been drawn at right angles?

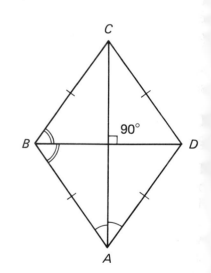

No matter what width ruler you used or what angle you used between your sets of parallels all the sides of your rhombuses will have the same length:

$$AB = BC = CD = DA.$$

If you now draw in the diagonals of any rhombus you will find that they are perpendicular

$$BD \perp AC.$$

Further, the diagonals bisect the angles at the corners which they join, for example

$$\angle BAC = \angle DAC \text{ and } \angle CBD = \angle DBA.$$

These properties are not generally true of other parallelograms and this can be neatly shown by contrasting what happens with a cut-out of a rhombus and of a non-special parallelogram when they are folded along their diagonals.

Because of the special properties of a rhombus and the ease with which it can be drawn using the parallel sides of a ruler it affords alternative ways of carrying out several of the traditional constructions which used a compass and straight edge.

Bisecting an angle

To bisect an angle such as $\angle ABC$, use a ruler to draw lines parallel to BC and BA, so that they intersect at P. Join BP to bisect the angle.

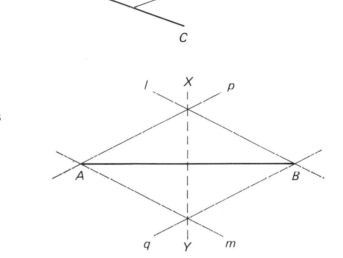

Bisecting a line segment

To bisect a line segment AB first position the ruler so that it lies from top left to bottom right with its edges just touching A and B and draw lines l and m. Now position the ruler so that it lies from top right to bottom left with its edges just touching A and B and draw in lines p and q.

These four lines now form a rhombus with AB as one of its diagonals. Draw in the second diagonal XY to bisect AB.

Construct a line at right angles to a given line

To draw a line through B which is perpendicular to AB first use your ruler to draw parallel lines x, y, z to obtain points M and N which are equidistant from B. Now with your ruler from top left to bottom right and its edges touching M and B draw the lines r and s. The rhombus formed by r, s, y and z is then such that its diagonal is perpendicular to AB.

Alternatively, having produced points M and N the line segment MN could be bisected as in the previous construction.

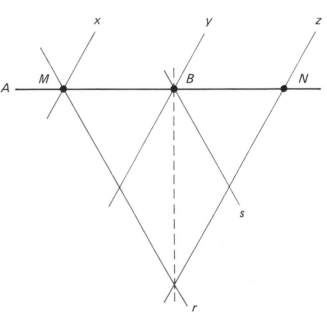

Problem: Given a mirror line and a point not on the line how would you construct its mirror image using just the parallel sides of a ruler?

94 Thwaites' conjecture

When Bryan Thwaites was a schoolmaster in the early 1950s he set his pupils a task of investigating the sequence of numbers produced when if a number was even it was halved and if it was odd it was multiplied by 3 and then increased by 1.

For example, if 7 is taken as the starting point then

$$7 \text{ odd } \rightarrow 7 \times 3 + 1 = 22$$
$$22 \text{ even } \rightarrow 22 \div 2 \quad = 11$$
$$11 \text{ odd } \rightarrow 11 \times 3 + 1 = 34$$
$$34 \text{ even } \rightarrow 34 \div 2 \quad = 17$$
$$17 \text{ odd } \rightarrow 17 \times 3 + 1 = 52$$
$$52 \text{ even } \rightarrow 52 \div 2 \quad = 26$$
$$26 \text{ even } \rightarrow 26 \div 2 \quad = 13$$

and so on.

Clearly an odd number leads to a larger number, but it will necessarily be even, so at the next stage it will be halved.

From the pupils' investigations at the time, and his own researches since, Bryan Thwaites believes that the sequence will eventually reach 1, at which point it would keep cycling through the sequence 421421421... so 1 can be taken as the end point. Many mathematicians around the world have tried to prove this conjecture, or alternatively find a different end point, but so far without success.

Continue the above sequence until it reaches 1 and then investigate the process with other starting points.

The process is summarised by the adjoining flow diagram.

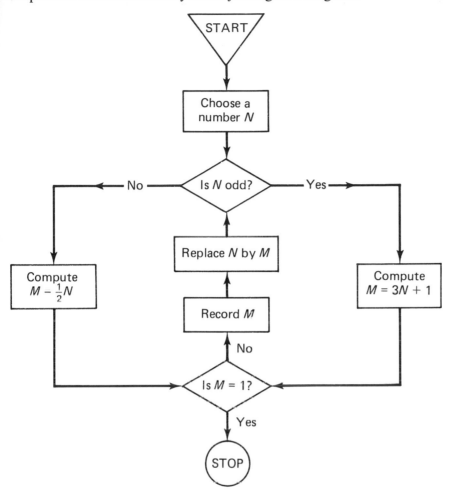

95 Cryptarithms and alphametic puzzles

Puzzles in which letters or symbols stand for digits, such as

```
            *  *  *
        _____
* * * ) *  *  *  *  *  *
        *  0  *  *
        _____
           *  *  *  *
           *  5  0  *
           _____
              *  *  *
              *  4  *
              _____
```

```
      B C
    × B C
    _____
    A B C
```

```
      A B C D D
    + B C E F D
    _____
      F E G H I B
```

are known as cryptarithms and their solution requires a mixture of analytical skills and trial and error. Such problems have long been popular but create even more interest when

103

the numbers involved are replaced by suitably related words
such as

$$
\begin{array}{r}
\text{S E N D} \\
+ \text{M O R E} \\
\hline
\text{M O N E Y}
\end{array}
\qquad \text{and} \qquad
\begin{array}{r}
\text{F I T} \\
- \text{M E N} \\
\hline
\text{J O G}
\end{array}
$$

when they are known as alphametic puzzles.

Ideally these puzzles should have a unique solution as do most of the above, but where there are more solutions such as with the last one mentioned the challenge is to find all the solutions.

Consider the slogan

$$
\begin{array}{r}
\text{M A R S} \\
+ \text{B A R S} \\
\text{A R E} \\
\hline
\text{B E S T}
\end{array}
$$

In trying to solve this one it is wise to start with the left-hand column where M + B + (carry digit) must equal B. This immediately tells us that M = 0 and that the carry digit from the hundreds column is zero. In turn we can see that this restricts the possibilities for A as three As cannot exceed 9. Over to you!

Making up successful alphametic puzzles is not easy. The following were attempts by the author after the 1985 Olympics

$$
\begin{array}{r}
\text{C R A M} \\
+ \quad \text{C O E} \\
\hline
\text{R A C E}
\end{array}
\qquad \text{and} \qquad
\begin{array}{r}
\text{C A R L} \\
+ \quad \text{L E W I S} \\
\hline
\text{W I N N E R}
\end{array}
$$

One of these has no solution, the other has several solutions.

Decide which is which and then state the values for E which make the solution unique.

96 Community coppers

A city police force has to keep its blocks of buildings under constant surveillance at night on all sides. The blocks are all the same size, square, and in a regular pattern as shown.

Each police constable can see only the length of one block. For example, a constable at A can see two sides of each of the four blocks which meet at that cross roads. A constable at B on the edge of the city can only watch two sides on each of two blocks however, while a constable at C could only watch two sides of one block.

The problem is to find the smallest number of police constables who could keep a watch on the above 4×3 city.

Investigate the number of constables required for cities of a different size and see if you can find any general patterns.

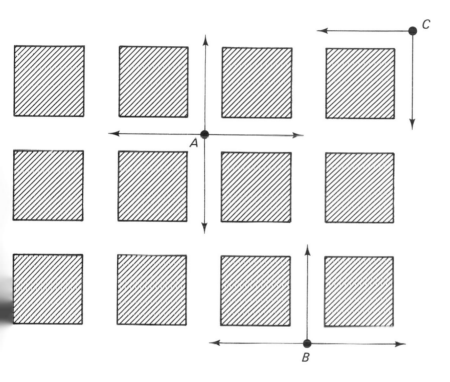

97 Exactly six primes

Using the digits $1, 2, 3, 4, 5, 6, 7, 8$ and 9 once, and only once, it is possible to make six prime numbers in a variety of ways. For example,

  2   5   7   43   61   89

If you allow yourself to use operations too then there are many possibilities such as

  2   3   5   7 $(8 + 9)$ $4 \times 6 - 1$

Investigate!

98 Magic polygons

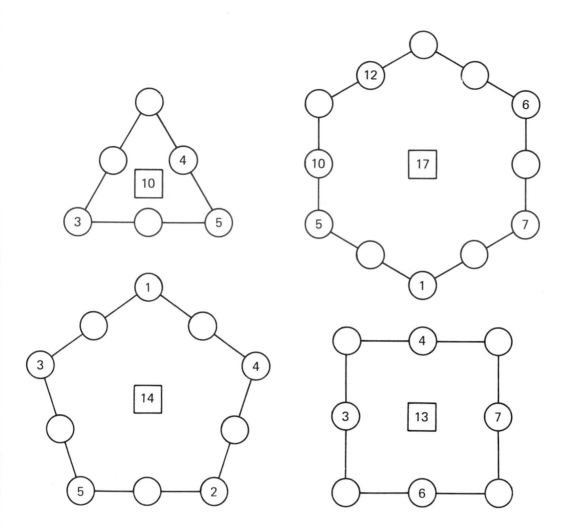

Complete these magic polygons by putting numbers in the circles so that the total along each side of the polygon is equal to the number given in the centre of each polygon. The numbers to be used for the triangle are 1 to 6, the numbers for the square 1 to 8, the numbers for the pentagon 1 to 10, and for the hexagon 1 to 12.

With the magic total given and many of the numbers already in place the solutions to the above polygons were relatively easy to find. The real problem is to try to find all the possible ways in which the same numbers could be put in the circles to make the polygons magic. The totals may not be the same, and there are at least four solutions in each case.

Investigate strategies for these polygons which could be used to search for solutions of polygons with more sides.

99 Quartering a circle

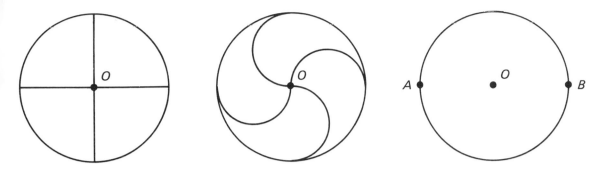

A circle can be divided into four parts of equal area in many
ways, two of which are shown above. See what other ways
you can find of doing this.

Now see if you can find a way of drawing three curves from
A to B, of equal length, which do not cross each other and
divide the circle above into four equal areas.

100 Sweeping the park efficiently

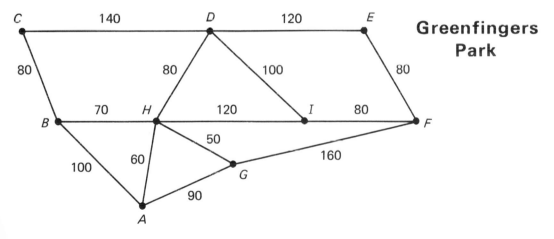

Greenfingers
Park

The map above shows the paths in an inner city park, with
their lengths given in metres. Each day before the park is
open to the public a council worker drives around all the
paths with a mechanical road sweeper. The sweeper is
housed at H and the worker is annoyed because no matter
what route is followed it does not seem possible to sweep all
the paths without retracing some. Is this inevitable?

What is the shortest distance which the sweeper can take to
sweep all the paths and return to H?

Can you find a general strategy for solving problems of this
type?

101 Connecting the fire hydrants

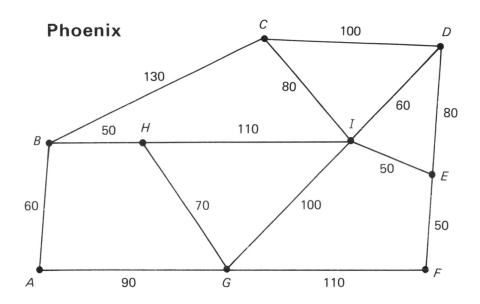

The town of Phoenix was notorious for the number of its houses that were lost due to fires. To overcome this bad reputation the town councillors drew up a plan to site nine fire hydrants at the points shown on the above map. To ensure sufficient water pressure at these hydrants it was decided to lay a new water main to interconnect them all. Digging trenches to put in the necessary pipes was going to be very expensive so the town councillors decided to hold a competition to see who could devise the shortest water main to connect all the hydrants. Because of the existing buildings the pipes could only be placed along the lines shown on the map. The length of each line in metres is given on the map.

Would you have won the competition?

102 Traffic engineering

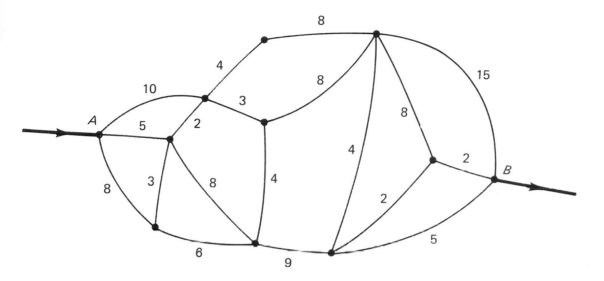

On holiday weekends the traffic passing through a
Westcountry town becomes chaotic. The main roads from
the seaside resorts all converge on the town at A (see the road
map above) and the main road to the Midlands leaves the
town at B. The numbers on the map show the maximum
capacity in hundreds of cars per hour of each section of road
in the town.

Supposing that the cars arriving at A use the roads to their
best advantage, what is the maximum possible flow of traffic
obtainable from A to B? How many roads could be
pedestrianised without affecting the maximum traffic flow
from A to B?

Suppose the road engineer has been told that there is
sufficient money to increase the capacity of one section of
road before the next holiday season, which section should be
modified and by how much? Will this modification have any
influence on any pedestrianisation plans?

103 The shunting yard

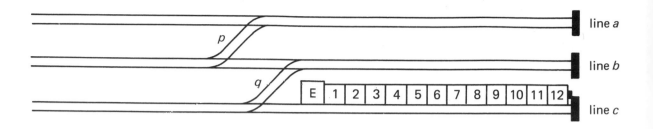

Three parallel tracks in a shunting yard, a, b and c, are connected by short tracks p and q. There are twelve trucks numbered 1 to 12 on line c, see the diagram, and it is required that trucks numbered 3, 7, 10 and 11 are shunted onto line a by the engine on line c to make up a train for a new destination. How would you do this in the most efficient way possible, that is with the fewest shunts? The remaining trucks and engine are to end up on line c.

104 Sort these out

(a) A computer programmer worked out the product of her age in years, the age of her cat in years, and the number of her house. Given that the product was 17 654 how old was she?

(b) When a teacher's telephone bill arrived she noticed with interest that the number of pounds was a factor of her telephone number. What's more, she realized that the remaining factors corresponded to the size of her fifth year mathematics class and to the number of her children.

Her telephone number was 18998 and you might be interested to know she had one more son than she had daughters.

What can you find out about her?

105 The ship's masts

Two ship's masts are of height 6 m and 4 m respectively. Guy wires are stretched from the top of each to the base of the other as shown. The wires cross at a height of 2.4 m above the deck.

How far apart are the masts?

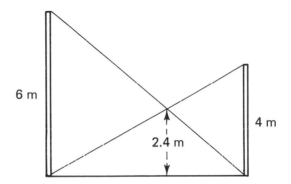

6 m

4 m

2.4 m

106 Complete the set

| 1 | 9 | 64 | 256 | 1296 | 2187 | 3125 | 4096 |

This series is incomplete. Spot the underlying pattern and supply the missing number.

107 1984 revisited

This activity has nothing to do with George Orwell!
(a) Did you know that $1985^2 - 1984^2$ is a perfect square? When did this last happen?
(b) It is not very difficult to express 1984 using eight '4' digits and any mathematical symbols you might care to use, but it will tax your ingenuity to do the same using four '8' digits.

108 Kirkman's schoolgirls problem

This problem was first proposed by
T.P. Kirkman in the *Lady's and
Gentleman's Diary* for 1850 and it
has since been subject to much analysis by numerous puzzlers
and mathematicians.

The puzzle concerns the house-mistress of a girls' boarding
school who took her 15 girls for a walk daily. They always
walked in crocodile in 5 rows with 3 abreast. From her
experience over many years the house-mistress had devised a
scheme whereby each girl had two different walking
companions on each day of the week.

Before trying this question try solving the similar one
applying to 9 boys walking in 3 rows with 3 abreast who are to
have different walking companions on 4 days.

109 Food for thought!

You will need your wits about you when considering the
following:

(*a*) A business man called away
in a hurry packed his bag in
the dark so as not to disturb
his wife. He had only two
colours of socks in his drawer
and, being a methodical
person, he knew the drawer
contained 10 grey socks and
14 brown socks.

How many socks did he take
out to be sure of getting a
pair to match?

(b) The row/column/diagonal total for a 3 × 3 magic square is 20. The first two entries are given, what are the remaining entries?

11	3	

(c) Let $x = y$ be any non-zero number. Then multiplying through by x gives

$$x^2 = xy$$

and subtracting y^2 gives

$$x^2 - y^2 = xy - y^2$$

factorising both sides leads to

$$(x - y)(x + y) = (x - y)y$$

and then dividing through by the common factor leaves

$$x + y = y$$

But $y = x$ so

$$2x = x$$

and as x is non-zero we must conclude that

$2 = 1$

Where is the flaw in the argument?

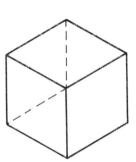

(d) Find the angle between the two dotted lines drawn on the faces of a cube.

(e) AB, BC and CA represent three runways at a busy airport. It is planned to site a new terminal building at a point P so that the total distance of the approach runways to be built

$$PN + PL + PM$$

is a minimum.
  ABC is an equilateral triangle, and the new runways are perpendicular to the main runways. Where should P be sited?

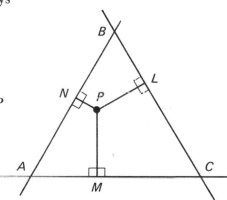

110   Think again!

```
1
1  1
2  1
1  2  1  1
1  1  1  2  2  1
3  1  2  2  1  1
1  3  1  1  2  2  2  1
```

What is the next line?

In which line does 4 occur first.

The step from one line to the next is very logical and not difficult, but can you spot it?

111   Nine Men's Morris

This is a very old game for two players. Records of it have been found in ancient Egypt, in Ceylon and in Greece. It has been played throughout Europe for many centuries with evidence accumulated from such differing sources as a Viking ship and a bronze age burial site in Ireland.

The game is played with counters (pebbles) on a board like that shown comprising 24 points connected by three concentric squares and four other median lines. Each player starts with 9 counters, a different colour for each player, and players take turns to place one of their counters on a vacant point.

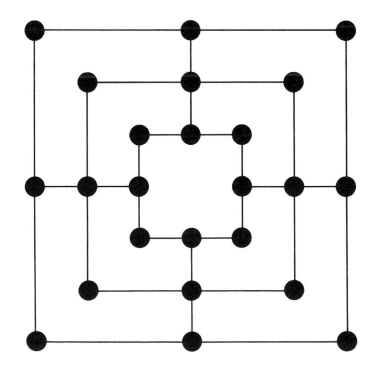

Every time a player forms a line of three connected counters (called a *mill*) an opponent's counter may be removed from the board. But note that counters forming a mill cannot be removed.

The *object* of the game is to immobilize the opponent's counters or to reduce them to just two.

When all of a player's counters have been placed on the board, a move consists of sliding one of these counters along a line to any adjacent vacant point. The object is still to complete a mill so that an opponent's counter can be removed and the opponent has less chance of being able to do the same in return.

Once a mill is established a player can break and remake it by moving one of the three counters to an adjacent point and back again in two moves.

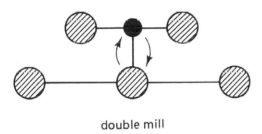

double mill

A very strong formation to try to bring about for oneself, but to prevent one's opponent making, is a *double mill*. This is a group of 5 counters, see the diagram, which enables the player to form a mill with every turn.

If you have never played this game it is time you had a go. The fact that it has survived for so long virtually unchanged says something. It has the advantage of being more demanding than 0s and Xs but offers the opportunity to be skilful without being too protracted. The game is available commercially in many forms, some with plastic pegs in a plastic board with others using colourful glass marbles on a wooden base. But why not make your own?

112 Some curious number relations

$$43 = 4^2 + 3^3$$
$$135 = 1^1 + 3^2 + 5^3$$
$$518 = 5^1 + 1^2 + 8^3$$
$$2427 = 2^1 + 4^2 + 2^3 + 7^4$$

See if you can find any more with similar patterns.

113 Squared sums!

D. St P. Barnard regularly sets puzzles in *The Daily Telegraph* and set one recently based on the intriguing relation

$$(6048 + 1729)^2 = 60\,481\,729$$

There is another pair of 4-digit numbers with the same property but without a microcomputer you may take a long time to find it. However similar properties exist for pairs of single-digit number and pairs of 2-digit numbers which are much more accessible. Investigate all the solutions to

$$(a + b)^2 = ab \quad \text{where } ab \text{ is a 2-digit number,}$$
$$(ab + cd)^2 = abcd \text{ where } abcd \text{ is a 4-digit number.}$$

114 Matrix manoeuvres

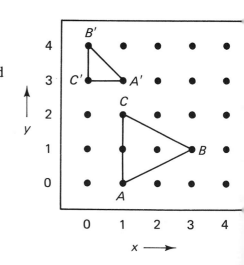

The 25 points on a 5×5 pinboard are identified by ordered pairs of numbers (x, y) as shown, where

$$x, y \in \{0, 1, 2, 3, 4\}.$$

Transformations are carried out on the pinboard by using 2×2 matrices and doing all the arithmetic modulo 5.

So, for example, the matrix $\begin{pmatrix} 1 & 2 \\ 3 & 0 \end{pmatrix}$ transforms

$\triangle ABC$ with $A(1,0)$, $B(3,1)$ and $C(1,2)$
to $\triangle A'B'C'$ with $A'(1,3)$, $B'(0,4)$ and $C'(0,3)$
as $\begin{pmatrix} 1 & 2 \\ 3 & 0 \end{pmatrix}\begin{pmatrix} 1 & 3 & 1 \\ 0 & 1 & 2 \end{pmatrix} = \begin{pmatrix} 1 & 0 & 0 \\ 3 & 4 & 3 \end{pmatrix}$ modulo 5.

The effect of different matrices can be investigated but the puzzle here is to find a matrix M so that, starting with $A(1,0)$, repeated multiplication by M will produce a succession of images A', A'' etc. which visit every pin of the pinboard except $(0,0)$ in turn.

115 Odds on winning

At a local point-to-point meeting one of the races had only four horses running and the odds offered by the bookmakers are those shown here. Odds of 5 to 2 mean that for every £2 bet the punter wins £5 and has the £2 bet returned, if this horse wins.

How could you lay your bets so that you could be sure that no matter which horse won you would win £10.

	Odds
Brigadoon	2 to 1 favourite
Tophatter	5 to 2
Lightning	6 to 1
Virginsky	6 to 1

116 Plans and elevations

Shown here are the plan and front elevation of a metal casting. Give a possible side elevation and sketch the resulting solid.

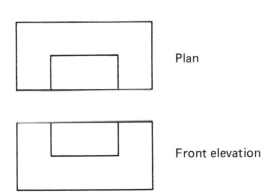

Plan

Front elevation

117 Thinking time

a) What is the angle between the hands of a clock at 3.12?
b) In every hour the minute hand coincides with the hour hand at some point. If, when they coincide, the hands are between 7 and 8, what is the time?

118 The Grand Prix circuit

The plan of a Grand Prix car racing circuit is as shown. Every time a car rounds a bend the wheels on the outside of the bend travel further than those on the inside. If the distance between the inner and outer wheels of a car is 2 metres, how much further do the outer wheels travel on one lap of this circuit?

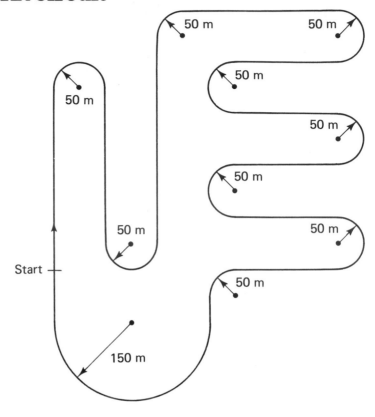

50 m

50 m

50 m

50 m

50 m

50 m

50 m

50 m

50 m

Start

50 m

150 m

119 Robotics

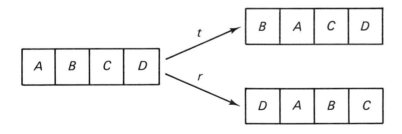

At a point on a production line four components arrive in order *ABCD* but may be required at the next stage in any order. To achieve the order required a robot has been programmed to do two basic operations:

  t: interchange the first two components
  r: move the last component to the front and push them all back one space.

These operations are represented by the diagram above.

How can the robot's two basic operations be used to produce the order *DACB*?

120 Improve your chances at Monopoly

Monopoly must be one of the best board games ever invented. It is played throughout the world. Its unique blend of luck and skill in the context of buying land and houses, where cash flow problems, income tax and mortgages feature, make it probably the first business game. When playing the game the position of your piece and your opponents' pieces, what you and they own, and where you and they are likely to land next is crucial. Are you going to be caught for exorbitant rent, or go to jail? To play the game well you need to have a good understanding of the probabilities of obtaining the different scores 2, 3, ... 12 when two dice are tossed.

The following discussion is based on the British board, but the strategy outlined will be the same whichever board is being used.

At the start of the game everyone is at GO and keen to land on property which they can buy. Stations are a favourite for many players, but how likely is it that you can land on King's Cross Station with your first turn? To get there you need a total of 5 from the two dice and this can be achieved in four ways. Imagine one dice is red and the other blue then the four ways are shown in the diagram.

4 + 1   3 + 2   2 + 3   1 + 4

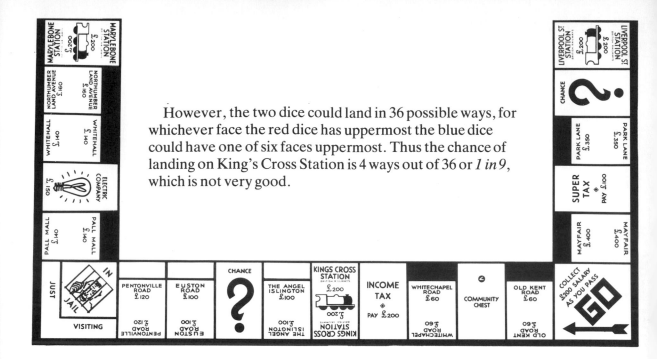

However, the two dice could land in 36 possible ways, for whichever face the red dice has uppermost the blue dice could have one of six faces uppermost. Thus the chance of landing on King's Cross Station is 4 ways out of 36 or *1 in 9*, which is not very good.

Suppose, however, you are keen to purchase one of the properties at the end of the first side, that is the blue sites, The Angel Islington, Euston Road or Pentonville Road. To get on one of these from GO you would need a total from the two dice of 6 or 8 or 9. Now there are fourteen ways of obtaining one of these totals

$$6 = 5 + 1 \text{ or } 4 + 2 \text{ or } 3 + 3 \text{ or } 2 + 4 \text{ or } 1 + 5$$
$$8 = 6 + 2 \text{ or } 5 + 3 \text{ or } 4 + 4 \text{ or } 3 + 5 \text{ or } 2 + 6$$
$$9 = 6 + 3 \text{ or } 5 + 4 \text{ or } 4 + 5 \text{ or } 3 + 6.$$

Hence the chance of landing on a blue property is 14 out of 36 which is getting on for 1 in 2, so is quite good.

In contrast, if you wanted to land on the Electric Company you would need a total of 12 which can only be achieved as a double 6 so giving a chance of *1 in 36*.

To find the chance of landing on any part of the board it is helpful to have a look at all the possible total which can be obtained by tossing two dice. The diagram here represents all the 36 ways in which the dice can land, with the numbers inside the square giving the corresponding totals. From this diagram you can see, for example, that a total of 7 occurs in six ways so the chance of getting this score would be 6 out of 36 or *1 in 6*.

With this diagram it is easy to answer such questions as 'If I am at Liverpool Street Station what is the chance that I will land on Super Tax or Income Tax in my next throw?'

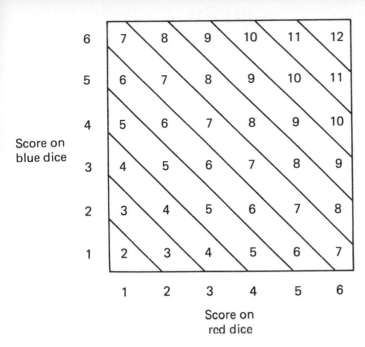

Score on
blue dice

Score on
red dice

The totals to land on these would be 3 and 9. Now the diagram shows that 3 can happen in two ways and 9 in four ways so the chances of landing would be 6 out of 36 or 1 in 6 again.

When you are playing Monopoly you are forever having to make decisions about spending money whether to buy a new site or build houses or hotels. These decisions will depend not only on the cash you have in hand, but on an assessment of what you may be paying out by landing on your opponents' property, and what income you may have by your opponents landing on yours. Having a better understanding of the chances of the different totals arising when tossing two dice increases the likelihood that a player will make better decisions.

Another area of Monopoly which bears mathematical analysis is to compare the rate of return for the same outlay on different properties. For example the addition of a second house to Pentonville Road costs £50 and the rent goes from £40 to £100 while the addition of a second house to Old Kent Road which also costs £50, only raises the rent from £10 to £30.

Is it better to spend one's money buying lots of different sites or to concentrate on one block and develop it fully. The way the rent climbs rapidly as a site is developed further would suggest the latter strategy. However it is important to accumulate sites initially as they can be used as bargaining power to complete the block you want, whether it be Mayfair and Park Lane or four Stations.

121 The cyclo-cross race

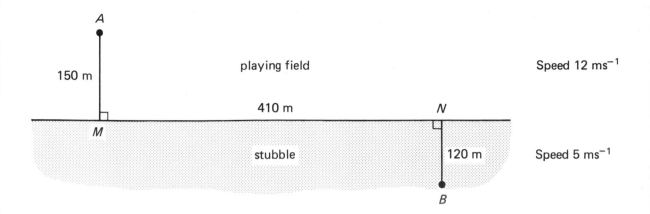

A

150 m

playing field

Speed 12 ms^{-1}

410 m

N

M

stubble

120 m

Speed 5 ms^{-1}

B

In a cyclo-cross race the cyclists enter a playing field at A. They have to cross this before crossing the stubble of a recently harvested cornfield and leaving it at a gate B. The boundary between the playing field and the cornfield is a straight line which can be crossed by the cyclists where they please. Now the cyclists hope to average 12 m s^{-1} across the playing field but only 5 m s^{-1} across the stubble. See the diagram.

   Where would you suggest the cyclists cross the boundary MN and how quickly should they be able to cycle from A to B?

122 Carving up the camels

On his deathbed the elderly arab gathered his three sons around him and expressed his wish that his 23 prize camels should be shared among them. Ahab the eldest was to have half of the camels, Aziz the second son was to have a third and Abdul the youngest was to have an eighth share. Initially pleased with their lot the sons soon realised they had a problem for they couldn't see how they could divide 23 camels into their allotted shares without slaughtering some of them. In their anguish they turned to their late father's revered brother for advice. After sleeping on the problem he lent them one of his own prize camels thus making a total of 24 and suggested they shared them out. Ahab took 12, his half share, Azis then took 8, his third, and Abdul then took 3, his eighth share, and then returned his uncle's camel to him with much thanks. Where is the catch?

123 The cranky calculator

An electronic calculator has all its digit keys and its memory key working efficiently but the only function keys still working reliably are

| + | | − | | x^2 |

Devise a routine which enables you to find the product of any two numbers – that is, numbers within the capacity of the calculator.

124 Calculator contortions

To test the ingenuity of her brightest pupils, Mrs Challenger set them the potentially dreary task of working out a long list of multiplications. But to help them she gave them each a calculator which had been especially modified so that the only keys still operational were the digit keys, the memory, and the function keys | + | | − | and | 1/x | . After an hour most of her pupils were defeated and resorted to long multiplication, but long before this Betty Bolzano, the form genius, had produced all the correct answers using one of the calculators. How did she do it?

125 The chocolate manufacturer's dilemma

A manufacturer of chocolates designed a new box of chocolates to celebrate the firm's centenary. The box was carefully designed to just hold 48 identical spherical chocolates arranged in a single layer with 8 rows of 6.

Unfortunately, when all the preparations were complete it was found that the chocolates were 4% below their advertised weight. It was too late to redesign the boxes and too difficult to change the specification for the chocolates. But there is a neat way in which the manufacturer can overcome the dilemma. How?

126   The squash match

After winning the semi-final of the local squash tournament the number one seed reflected on how lucky he had been. After a good first game the second game was disastrous and he had only just scraped home in the third before rounding off the match in the fourth game as he had begun. He realised that his points total was identical to his opponent's and a perfect number. What was the points score in each game?

127   Toilet tissue thickness

An accountant was always on the lookout for a bargain when she did her shopping. One day she saw that Sainsbury's had a special line selling packs with 4 rolls of toilet tissues, with 240 sheets in each roll. Knowing how particular her sons were about the thickness of the tissues they liked to use, she tried to work out the thickness of these particular tissues so that she could compare them with those she usually purchased.

She knew the tissues were 14 cm long and she estimated the diameter of the rolls as 11 cm, each wound on cardboard cylinders of diameter 4 cm. At first she was concerned at the fact that the tissues were wound onto the roll in a spiral with increasing radius, but it wasn't long before she saw her way around this problem and calculated the tissue's thickness. How thick was the tissue?

About how many turns of paper are there on each roll?

128 Stop the gaps

The following sequences are all derived from one
well-known one. Spot the patterns and stop the gaps!
(a) 2, 5, 10, 17, −, 41, 58.
(b) 2, 6, 30, 210, −, 30030.
(c) 5, 8, 12, 18, −, −, 36.

129 Multiplication squares

×	3	2	8	9
5				
4				
6				
11				

×	a	b	c	d
p	63			36
q	56		24	
r		22		8
s			30	

Finding different ways of reinforcing number facts is
important throughout school for many children. The
multiplication square on the left presents 16 multiplication
facts in an order which doesn't correspond to the tables so
some thought is required. Children will much more readily
fill in a square of this kind than do the multiplications it
entails if they are set as separate sums – and of course they are
easy to set!
  The table on the right is of the same kind but is more of a
challenge. Here a sufficient number of the products is given
to enable the numbers a, b, c, d, p, q, r, s bordering the
square to be deduced before completing the table.
  In setting these there is no reason why the same number
cannot appear both on the top and the side, in fact if this is
avoided then the square of a number will never occur.
  Multiplication 'squares' can of course be 'rectangles'.

130 Reinforcing the number line

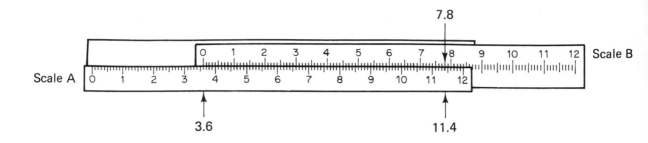

One of the keys to children's understanding of number is to help them to have an image of the numbers along a line as with a ruler. The addition of two numbers can then be seen as the addition of two lengths along the number line. This can be done by using two scales one on each of two rulers, but is better seen by making a slide rule from thin card as shown above. Some children can mark out their own scales but for most children it is probably better to photocopy a set of accurate scales.

To add 3.6 to 7.8, for example, first find the 3.6 mark on scale A (the fixed scale) and move the sliding scale B until the zero is immediately above it as in the above diagram. Next find 7.8 on scale B and note the number immediately below it on scale A, 11.4. This last number is the required sum, 3.6 + 7.8.

With the scales set in the position shown it is possible to read off very rapidly the sum of 3.6 and any number from 0 to 8.4 – the limitation being the length of the scale.

With an understanding of place value the same setting could also give the answers to additions such as

$$36 + 78, \qquad 360 + 290, \qquad 0.36 + 0.47.$$

The same slide rule can also give the answer to subtraction. Suppose, for example, we want to find 11.4 − 7.8.

The method is as follows.

(1) Find 11.4 on scale A.
(2) Find 7.8 on scale B and move the slide until the 7.8 is immediately above the 11.4 on scale A.
(3) The required difference is then the number on the A scale below the 0 on the B scale, 3.6.

Note as the slide is set in the diagram above all the numbers on scale A are 3.6 larger than the numbers on scale B opposite to them.

When the number line is extended to include the negative numbers, a similar slide rule can be constructed, but with 0 in the middle of each scale as shown above. The method for

126

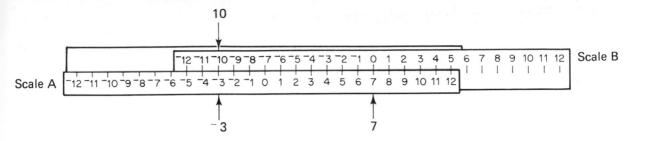

adding and subtracting directed numbers on this rule is exactly the same as adding the decimals on the first rule.

The rule is shown doing the calculation

$$7 + {}^-10 = {}^-3.$$

The method:
(1) Find 7 on scale A.
(2) Slide scale B until the 0 is immediately above the 7.
(3) Find $^-10$ on scale B and read off the number on scale A below it, $^-3$.

The same setting also shows how to calculate

$$^-3 - {}^-10 = 7$$

The method
(1) Find $^-3$ on scale A.
(2) Slide scale B until the $^-10$ on it is immediately above the $^-3$.
(3) Find the 0 on scale B and read off the number on scale A below it, 7.

Make up slide rules for yourself and you will see how well it helps towards seeing the negative numbers as an extension of the natural numbers.

131 A fascinating family of square numbers

$$
\begin{array}{rcl}
1\ 6 & = & 4^2 \\
1\ 1\ 5\ 6 & = & 34^2 \\
1\ 1\ 1\ 5\ 5\ 6 & = & 334^2 \\
1\ 1\ 1\ 1\ 5\ 5\ 5\ 6 & = & 3334^2 \\
1\ 1\ 1\ 1\ 1\ 5\ 5\ 5\ 5\ 6 & = & 33334^2
\end{array}
$$

Each number in this sequence is obtained from the previous one by inserting 15 in the middle like the extra leaf in an expanding table. Can you show why the numbers in this sequence will always be square no matter how far you go.

There is one other sequence of numbers like this one. See if you can find it.

132 Windscreen wiping

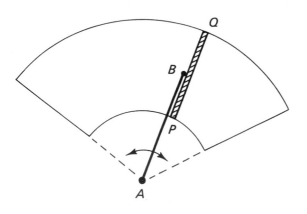
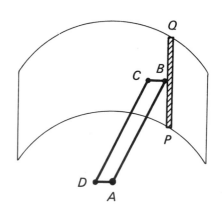

Investigate the area swept out by a windscreen wiper blade
PQ when attached to a typical car windscreen wiper arm *AB*,
and when attached to a parallelogram mechanism as seen on
many lorries and coaches. Assume that *B* is the mid-point of
PQ.

133 Intersecting circles

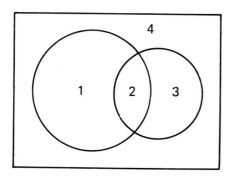
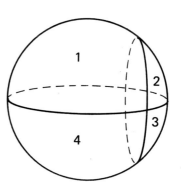

No matter how you draw two intersecting circles on a piece of
paper or on the surface of a sphere the effect is to divide the
surface into four distinct regions.

There is at least one surface, however, on which you can
draw two intersecting circles leaving the surface as *one*
interconnected region. Explain!

Commentary

1 Three-dimensional noughts and crosses

This is an excellent game for children to play to give spatial experience. It can be played just using counters on 4 × 4 square grids drawn on a piece of paper representing the four levels, but this is too difficult for all but the most intelligent children.

A peg in a corner controls 7 lines.

A peg on the edge of the grid controls 4 lines.

A peg on the inside of a square face of the cube controls 4 lines.

A peg on any one of the four holes inside the cube controls 7 lines.

There are 76 possible lines of four pegs. (On each level there are 8 lines parallel to the edges together with 2 diagonals – 10 horizontal lines on each level – 40 in all. Then there are 16 vertical lines, 4 long diagonals, and 2 diagonals in each of eight vertical planes.)

The minimum number of pegs to block all the lines appears to be 19.

On any level all the horizontal lines can be blocked by using just four pegs in one of the two ways shown here. The first of these, with its line of symmetry, is tempting to use but 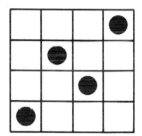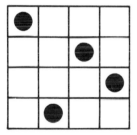 is soon seen to be inefficient. The second pattern, however, if employed suitably on each level will block all but three of the long diagonals. Three pegs can then be added to block them to give the total of 19. This solution, however, lacks the symmetry which is often found in problems of this kind, so the author hopes that someone might find a more satisfying one, even one with a smaller number of pegs.

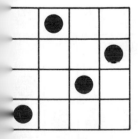

Level 1

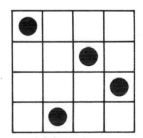

Level 2

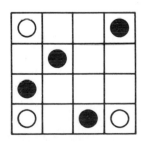

Level 3

Level 4

2 Don't be square

When this investigation is set to pupils without showing any examples of the squares to be found they almost always give an answer of 30 or fewer squares. It is the exceptional pupil who appreciates that squares can be obtained where sides are not parallel to the grid. Ask a class to draw a square and see how many draw it at an angle to the page. How often as teachers do we draw a square at an angle? There are in fact 50 possible squares to be found altogether as shown in the diagrams.

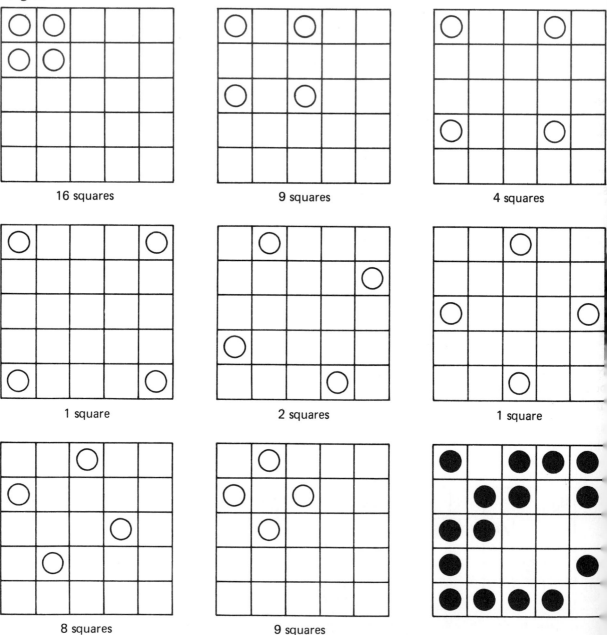

16 squares

9 squares

4 squares

1 square

2 squares

1 square

8 squares

9 squares

It is possible to put fifteen counters on the board so that no four lie at the vertices of a square. One solution is shown here, but it is not unique. This activity could be extended by, for example, looking at different-sized boards, or looking at parallelograms instead of squares. Related ideas can be found in *Mathematical Activities*, activities 95 and 106.

3   One-upmanship!

Yes, she is right. If $n_1, n_2, \ldots, n_8$ are consecutive numbers then $n_1^2 + n_4^2 + n_6^2 + n_7^2 = n_2^2 + n_3^2 + n_5^2 + n_8^2$ is always true.

Let the first number be n then the others will be $n+1, n+2, \ldots, n+7$.

Now

$$n^2 + (n+3)^2 + (n+5)^2 + (n+6)^2 = 4n^2 + 28n + 70$$

and

$$(n+1)^2 + (n+2)^2 + (n+4)^2 + (n+7)^2 = 4n^2 + 28n + 70$$

thus proving that Elizabeth was right.

However, the result is more general than she realised for it will also hold for any eight numbers in arithmetic progression such as

$$1, 4, 7, 10, 13, 16, 19, 22.$$

Is there a similar result for the squares of six consecutive numbers?

4   Which rectangles are possible?

No smaller square can be made. A 2×2 is clearly not possible and a 3×3 with an area of 9 square units cannot be made from tiles of area 4 square units.

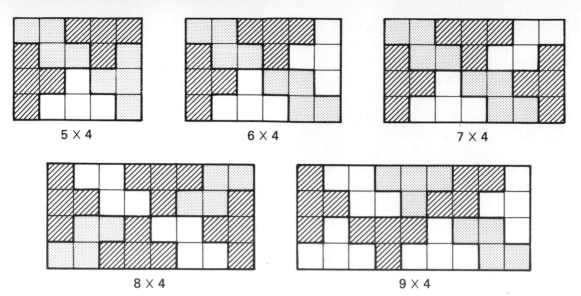

5 × 4   6 × 4   7 × 4

8 × 4   9 × 4

The diagrams above give solutions to the 5 × 4, 6 × 4, 7 × 4, 8 × 4 and 9 × 4 rectangles. The first three of these show how one solution develops from a previous one while the 8 × 4 shows how half turn symmetry has been exploited. The solutions are not unique. For example, a different 9 × 4 solution could be obtained by putting the 5 × 4 solution next to the 4 × 4 solution. All $n \times 4$ rectangles are possible for $n \geq 4$ as is easily seen by putting together combinations of the solutions given.

As the tiles have an area of 4 unit squares, only shapes of area $4n$ unit squares need be considered. This rules out the 5 × 3 and 6 × 5 rectangles as well as the rectangle with area 210 unit squares.

5 Inside and out

The fact is the hoops can be anywhere as long as the four smaller hoops do not overlap each other. The area inside a circle of radius 50 cm is 2500π cm^2. The total area inside the four circles of radius 40 cm, 20 cm, 20 cm and 10 cm is

$$(1600\pi + 400\pi + 400\pi + 100\pi) = 2500\pi \, \text{cm}^2$$

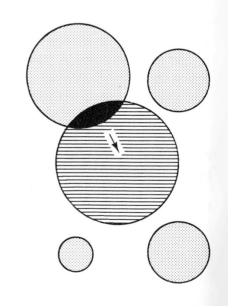

which is identical to the large circle. Start with all of the smaller hoops outside the large hoop, when the shaded areas clearly balance. Now imagine the 40 cm radius hoop moving towards the large hoop and overlapping it. The overlapping area is then lost to the 40 cm hoop and is also lost to the large hoop, so the balance of the shaded areas is maintained. The same argument applies if the other hoops overlap the large one so there is no difficulty in obtaining a balance!

6   A matchstick miscellany

In solving matchstick puzzles most people start with a hit or miss approach, but a little bit of analysis can pay dividends. In (a) there are 24 matches so removing 4 leaves 20. If exactly five identical squares have to be formed then it indicates the need to look for five squares which have no matchstick in common. As matches are only being removed, the arrangement must already exist within the original array and the solution is shown below. The smallest number of matches that can be removed to leave just two squares is eight.

In (b) four matches have to be moved so the number of matches in the solution is twelve, the same as at the start. Again, as three identical squares are to be formed we are looking for three squares with no matchstick common to two squares. From the starting point, five solutions at first seem possible, see figure (b), but only the last three are solutions as the others require that more than four matches are moved. It is also possible to form three identical squares by moving only three matches. Can you see how?

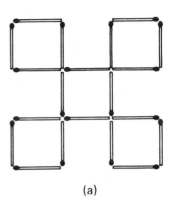

(a)

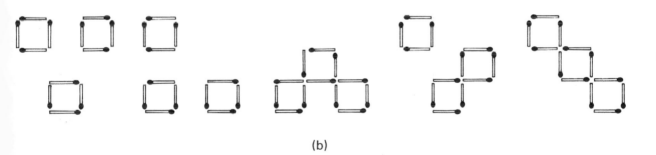

(b)

In (c) it is important to appreciate that the question does not ask for three *identical* equilateral triangles. A satisfying puzzle to solve.

NB Half length drinking straws are a useful aid in solving these puzzles, and safer than matches.

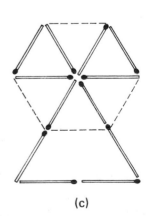

(c)

133

7 Coin contortions

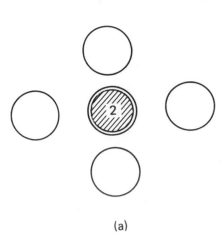

(a)

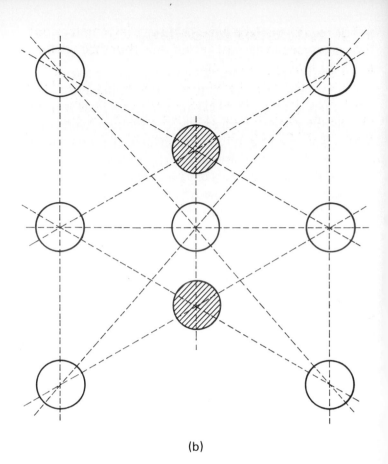

(b)

(a) The bottom coin of the
cross is moved on top of
the centre coin.

(b) The two coins are added
to the H pattern to give
ten lines of three coins as
shown.

8 An elephantine hole

Take a folded sheet of newspaper and make cuts as shown in
the diagram alternately from the folded edge and the edge
opposite the fold. Then cut along the fold line from P to Q.
The result is a long loop of newspaper. By making a sufficient
number of cuts theoretically the loop can be made as large as
one pleases and certainly large enough for an elephant!

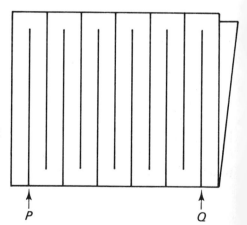

9 Octagonal operations

The paper folding approach brings out the innate symmetry
of the regular octagon. This could be accentuated by cutting
holes in the paper when folded and investigating the pattern
which is revealed when the paper is unfolded.

The regular octagon has eight lines of symmetry: four through opposite pairs of vertices and four through the mid-points of opposite sides.

The solutions to the puzzle dissections are as shown. The angle of 65° to construct the second one is a good approximation which makes this a practical possibility. The reader is left to work out the exact angle.

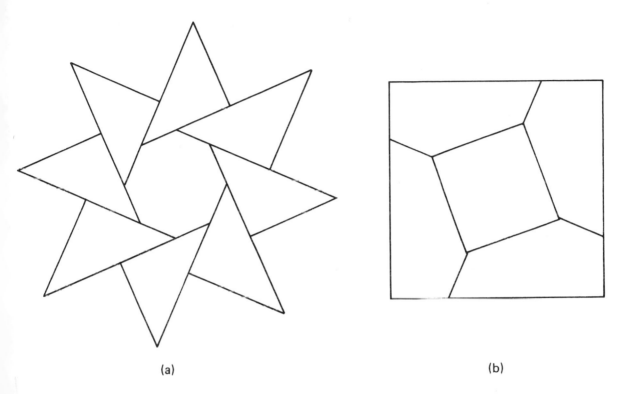

(a)   (b)

10   Delving into dissections

Figure (i) shows how the second dissection of the Greek cross can be found by superimposing the tessellation of squares over that of the crosses.

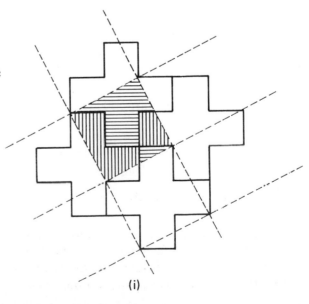

(i)

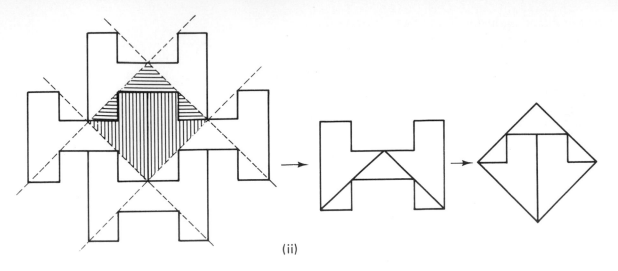

(ii)

Figure (ii) shows one way of fitting the squares over the H shapes to find a suitable dissection.

The cross shape fits neatly into a tessellation and when the centres of the crosses are joined they give a square tessellation which elegantly dissects the cross into four congruent pieces, see figure (iii).

The T shape, because of its lack of symmetry, poses a harder problem, but the tessellations shown in figure (iv) lead to a variety of dissections and two of those have been highlighted.

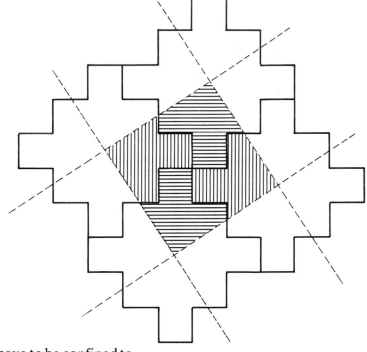

(iii)

This tessellation technique does not have to be confined to rectilinear figures as (v) shows. Here the vase shape tessellates and allows a neat way of superimposing a network of squares which in turn shows how the vase can be dissected with two straight cuts into four pieces which can be rearranged into a square. (See also *Mathematical Activities*, activity 86.)

All twelve pentominoes (*Mathematical Activities*, activity 76) will tessellate, so form a good starting point for shapes to dissect into pieces which will form squares. But see what else you can discover, the possibilities are limitless.

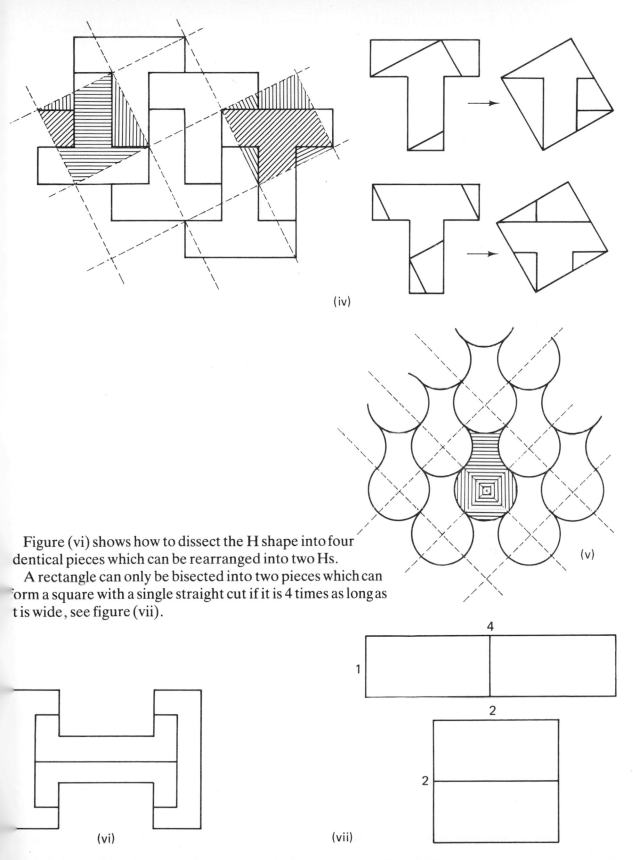

(iv)

(v)

Figure (vi) shows how to dissect the H shape into four identical pieces which can be rearranged into two Hs.

A rectangle can only be bisected into two pieces which can form a square with a single straight cut if it is 4 times as long as it is wide, see figure (vii).

(vi)

(vii)

137

However some other rectangles can be divided into two pieces by a stepped cut so that a square can be formed as with the 16 × 9 rectangle, see figure (viii). On which other rectangles can this method be used?

The solutions to Sam Loyd's dissection are shown in figure (ix).

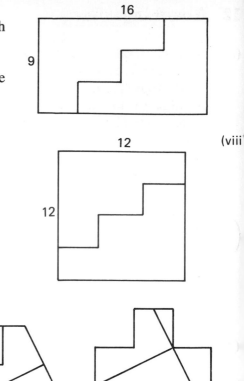

(viii)

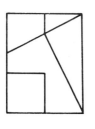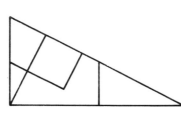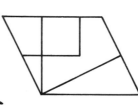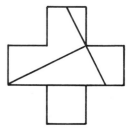

(ix)

Further ideas may be found in:
Madachy's Mathematical Recreations by J.S. Madachy
Recreational Problems in Geometric Dissections and How to Solve Them by H. Lindgren, revised by G. Frederickson
Puzzles and Curious Problems by H.E. Dudeney
Further Mathematical Diversions by Martin Gardner

11 The jeweller's chain

There are seven pieces to join so the obvious solution would appear to be to cut a link on six of the pieces and use it to add another piece of the chain thus taking 2 hours.

A better solution is to cut all the links of the piece which had 5 links and use those links to join together the remaining six pieces thus taking 1 hour and 40 minutes.

The best solution however is to cut the 4 links of the two pieces which had 2 links and use these to join together the remaining five pieces thus needing only 1 hour and 20 minutes.

The jeweller could thus have gone home at 6.20 pm.

12 Touching coins

(a) The usual solution given to this puzzle is to have three coins touching each other in an equilateral triangle array with the fourth coin on top of them. The most satisfying solution is to have the four coins placed as if they are the incircles of the faces of a regular tetrahedron.

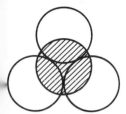
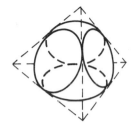

(b) A tricky puzzle to solve! First place two coins touching each other flat on top of a third coin as shown. Now stand two coins on the bottom coin and tilt them, to touch each other. With care the 'standing' coins can be placed to touch all three horizontal coins thus solving the problem.

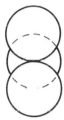

13 Two wrongs make a right

This is just one of the hundreds of puzzles set by the Victorian king of puzzles Henry Ernest Dudency. It has more than one solution. Four are given here

25938	25387	25469	49265
+ 25938	+ 25387	+ 25469	+ 49265
51876	50764	50938	98530

Another of his puzzles is based on the addition sum, below,

```
    FLY
+   FOR
  YOUR
  LI FE
```

in which each letter stands for a different digit and it is given that O stands for zero and I stands for one. The unique solution is given by

$$F = 5, L = 9, Y = 8, R = 7, U = 4, E = 2$$

14 Micro millions

$$1\,000\,000\,000 = 10^9 = 2^9 \times 5^9$$
$$= 512 \times 1\,953\,125$$

Any other factorisation will involve $2 \times 5 = 10$ and so involve a zero digit. With the usual price of micros being in hundreds of pounds the conclusion is that 1 953 125 micros were sold at £512.

A related investigation is to see which powers of 10 can be expressed as the product of two factors, neither of which contains a zero digit. 10^{10} cannot be so expressed, for example, as $2^{10} = 1024$.

15 The economy cut

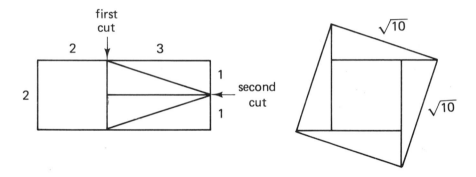

Feel pleased if you managed it with four cuts but congratulate yourself if you managed it in three cuts like Emma.

She first cut off a 2×2 square then cut the remaining rectangle into two 3×1 rectangles. Next she superimposed one of these rectangles on the other and cut along a diagonal to give herself four identical triangles which fitted neatly around the 2×2 square to form a $\sqrt{10} \times \sqrt{10}$ square. No doubt she lost some size in sewing the pieces together but the square she obtained would cover her 3×3 table.

16 The area of a parallelogram

These models may take a lesson to make but their impact on the pupils is far more than a formal proof of the result. Have your own larger demonstration model but do let pupils make their own.

17 Quadreels

This is a good game to play and increase spatial insight so it is worth making. Collecting enough cotton reels of the same kind may take a time but an alternative approach to making the pieces would be to cut slices off a garden hose.

See also activity 1, Three-dimensional noughts and crosses.

18 Folding 60° angles

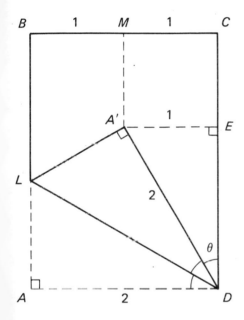

To see why the line LD is at 60° to DC, consider the diagram. Suppose $BC = AD = A'D$ are of length 2 units. Then $A'E = MC$ so is of length 1 unit. Thus in $\triangle A'DE$

$$\sin \theta = \tfrac{1}{2}$$

from which

$$\theta = 30°.$$

Hence

$$\angle ADA' = 60°.$$

Now $\angle ADL = \angle A'DL$ due to the fold, so they must each be 30°. Hence

$$\angle LDC = 60°.$$

The sequence of diagrams below shows how a regular hexagon can be folded from a square.

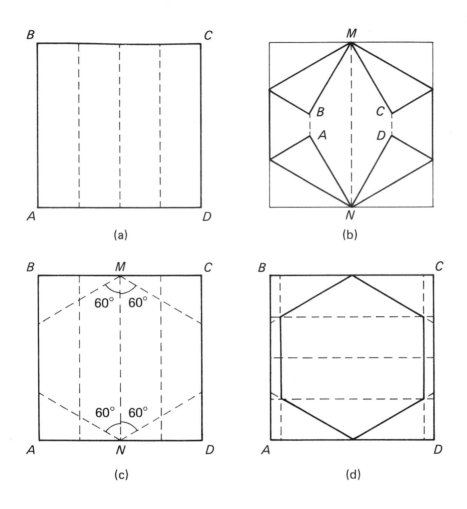

(a)

(b)

(c)

(d)

First, fold the paper into quarters by folding parallel to *AB*, see (a). Next fold in corners *A*, *B*, *C* and *D* from the mid-points *M* and *N* of sides *BC* and *AD* to form 60° angles as shown in (b) and (c). The hexagon which can be seen at this stage has the correct angles, 120°, but its sides are not all of equal length. One way to adjust this is to fold the square in quarters parallel to *BC*, and where the horizontal folds cut the slanting lines will give the positions of the vertices required, see (d).

19   Megalithic mathematics

The shapes discussed here are interesting in themselves and
satisfying to construct apart from their connection with stone
circles. Elliptical shapes also occur but these have been
omitted here as they were discussed in some detail in
Mathematical Activities and *More Mathematical Activities*.

Much of the original work on this topic was done by
Professor Thom, but for a very readable account with many
practical details you should read *Sun, Moon and Standing
Stones* by J.E. Wood.

For anyone particularly interested in theories about
Stonehenge then Gerald Hawkins' book *Stonehenge
Decoded* is compulsive reading.

20   Loading the ferry

Using the 'fill each lane from the left' strategy only 11 will be
loaded:

left lane $3 + 5 + 9 + 14 + 6 = 37$
middle lane $10 + 11 + 13 \quad = 34$
right lane $7 + 8 + 15 \quad = 30.$

This leaves spaces at the ends of the lanes of lengths 3 m, 6 m
and 10 m which cannot be utilised by the next vehicle in the
queue which is 11 m long. The percentage wastage is thus

$$\frac{(3 + 6 + 10)}{120} \times 100 \simeq 16\%$$

However, by carefully selecting the lane which each vehicle
joins as it enters the loading bay it is possible to load 13
vehicles with no wasted space:

3,   5,   9,   14, 6,   10, 11, 13, 7,   8,   15, 11, 8,   4
L   L   M   R   R   L   L   R   R   M   M   L   M

left lane $3 + 5 + 10 + 11 + 11 = 40$
middle lane $9 + 8 + 15 + 8 \quad = 40$
right lane $14 + 6 + 13 + 7 \quad = 40.$

21 A symmetric cross-number puzzle

The symmetry about the two lines at 45° automatically generates all the symmetry of a square so by the time all the black squares are filled in there are only a limited number of spaces to be filled. Because of the symmetry required the 2-digit number around the central square must be of the form xx, and to be prime must be 11. Similarly it can be argued that the number bordering each edge must be of the form $xyyx$. Such a number must have 11 as a factor so cannot be prime. It must therefore be $11^3 = 1331$. The remaining squares require pairs of numbers of the form xy and yx which are both prime such as 13 and 31, 17 and 71, and 37 and 73.

One solution is shown and three others are possible using the alternative corners given below.

The solution could have been made unique by adding the condition that one digit only appeared four times in the solution.

To show that a number of the form $xyyx$ must always have 11 as a factor note that

$$1000x + 100y + 10y + x = 1001x + 110y$$
$$= 11(91x + 10y)$$

This suggests an interesting investigation in itself, taking the factors of $abba$ as the starting point.

144

22 A question of place value

They both have the same sum. To see this without doing an addition sum note that in the column corresponding to 10^n there are either $(n+1)$ digits equal to $(9-n)$ or $(9-n)$ digits equal to $(n+1)$.

For example in the 10^2 column there are either 3 digits equal to 7 or 7 digits equal to 3. The result is that corresponding columns always have the same total.

23 Another number pattern

One way of seeing why the pattern works is to realise that for example

$$1234 = 1111 + 111 + 11 + 1$$

then

$$
\begin{aligned}
(1234 \times 8) + 4 &= (1111 \times 8) + (111 \times 8) + (11 \times 8) + (1 \times 8) + 4 \\
&= 8888 \quad + 888 \quad + 88 \quad + 8 \quad + 4 \\
&= (10\,000 - 1111) + (1000 - 111) + (100 - 11) + (10 - 1) \\
&= 11\,110 - 1111 - 111 - 11 - 1 \\
&= 9999 - (111 + 11 + 1) \\
&= 9999 - 123 \\
&= 9876
\end{aligned}
$$

24 The L-game

This game was devised by Edward de Bono to develop thinking skills and is discussed at length in his book *The Five-Day Course in Thinking*. It is an excellent way to develop children's ability to manipulate shapes in space as well as problem-solving and game-winning strategies.

25 One hundred up!

To work out a winning strategy start with the end point 100. If you can call 89 your opponent cannot reach 100 in his next turn but must put you in range of a win. So how can you put yourself in a position to call 89? If you go back 11 to 78 the same argument holds. Call 78 and your opponent must put you in range of 89 without being able to get there. So how can you put yourself in a position to call 78? The answer of course is to go back 11 to 67 … and then back 11 to 56 and so on.

The critical sequence is thus

1, 12, 23, 34, 45, 56, 67, 78, 89.

As soon as your opponent makes a call which is not in this sequence you will be able to call one of these numbers and then follow the sequence home to 100. Unless your opponent is aware of this strategy your chances of winning must be very high.

26 Mancala

This game does not need elaborate equipment as the Africans have demonstrated. At one level it requires no more than the ability to count and take pot luck on any gains, but clearly it can be played with much more skill and foresight.

For a detailed history of the game see *A History of Board Games* by H.J.R. Murray.

27 Tsyanshidzi

There are many critical positions to be avoided and/or brought about. For example if player *A* leaves the position (3,5) then this forces a win no matter what the opponent *B* does. *B* has eight choices but they all lead to disaster.

A leaves	*B* leaves	*A* leaves
	(2,5)	(2,1)
	(3,4)	(1,2)
(3,5)	(1,5)	(1,2)
	(3,3)	(0,0) Wins
	(0,5)	(0,0) Wins
	(2,4)	(2,1)
	(1,3)	(1,2)
	(0,2)	(0,0) Wins

Similar winning positions are (4,7), (6,10), (8,13), (9,15). Analyse them and see what others you can find.

28 Intersecting lines

This is a good investigation with many spatial spin-offs.

With n lines it is possible to obtain a maximum of $\frac{1}{2}n(n-1)$ intersections (each line can intersect $n-1$ others but intersections get counted twice). All lines parallel gives no intersections; all lines through one point is also possible; but after that the smaller numbers of intersections are not possible. With n lines it is possible to obtain $n-1$ intersections by having $n-1$ lines parallel and the other across them, and from $n-1$ to $\frac{1}{2}n(n-1)$ all solutions are possible. Some further solutions for 5 lines are shown below.

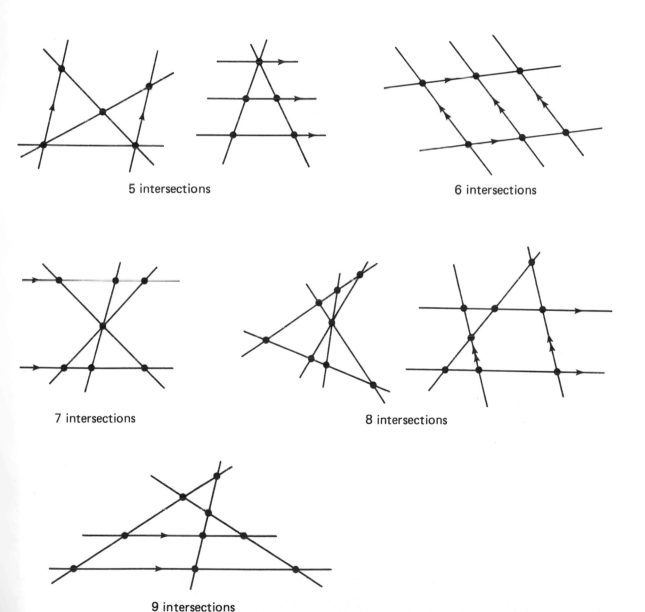

5 intersections

6 intersections

7 intersections

8 intersections

9 intersections

One solution to the last problem is to have a set of five parallel lines crossing a set of four parallel lines to give 20 intersections, and the 10th line through one of these points of intersection cutting the other seven lines.

Another neat solution is to have two intersecting pencils of five lines.

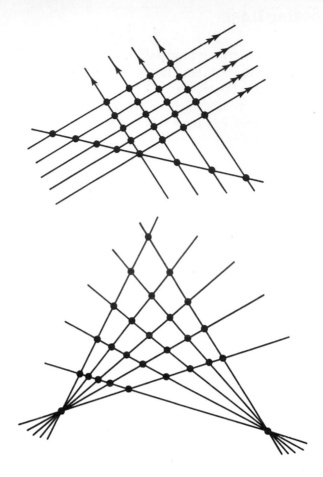

29   Make a rectangle

As a square made of pentominoes must have $(5n)^2$ squares the smallest possibility is a 5×5 but this can soon be seen to be impractical. The next to consider is a 10×10 and this is easily made but not with the six shapes Rachel was limited to.

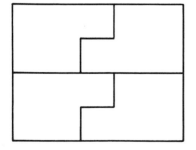 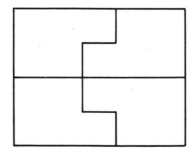 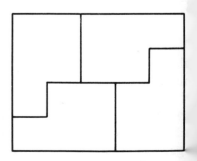

5 × 4 rectangles

148

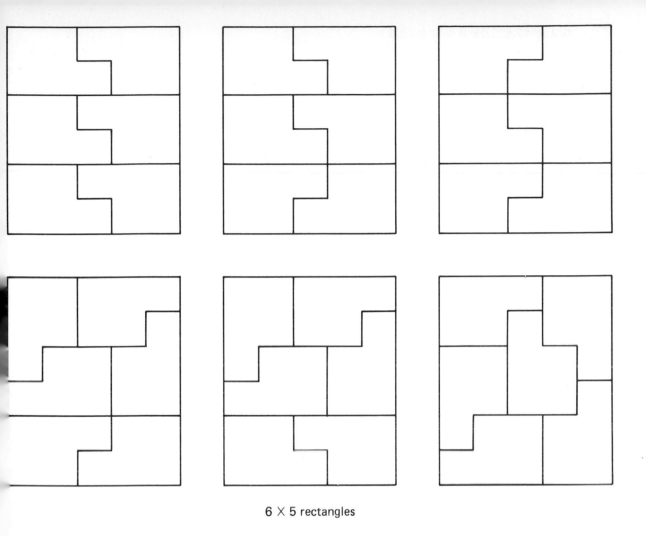

6 × 5 rectangles

30 As easy as abc!

$$2^5 \times 9^2 = 2592$$

31 The dishonest gold exporter

The customs officer weighed together 1 ingot from the first pile, 2 ingots from the second pile, 3 ingots from the third pile, …, 10 ingots from the tenth pile. Altogether 55 ingots whose legal weight is known. If the fourth pile contains the light ingots then the total weight of the 55 ingots will be 4 g below their legal weight. The number of grams below the legal weight will always indicate which is the pile of fraudulent ingots in a consignment. A neat solution!

32   Billy Bunter's bargain

He was able to collect 10 free bars.

Using 64 of the 71 labels collected he obtained eight free bars.

But each of these bars had a label which enabled him to collect one more free bar. With the label from this bar and the seven left from the original 71 he could then collect his tenth bar. Inevitably he had one label from that bar left which he kept to remind him of his lucky break!

33   All touching

This may seem an impossible problem to solve until you see the solution, (a).

Even more surprising is the ability to arrange seven pencils so that they all touch each other; see (b).

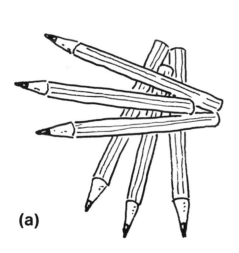

(a)

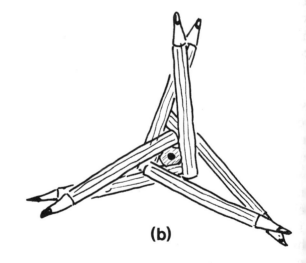

(b)

34   Mechanism miscellany

There is much scope here for observation, analysis, model-making and invention. Much can be achieved with card and paper fasteners but, for more intricate mechanisms, Meccano, Fischertechnik and Lego kits give more scope. When you get your eye in there is no end to the mechanisms to be seen and their study is very rewarding. See *Machines, Mechanisms and Mathematics* by the author if in the school library. Many interesting books are now available such as

Machines, an Illustrated History by Sigvard Strondh
How Things Work, The Universal Encyclopaedia of Machines by C. van Amerongen
Mechanism Design, An Introductory Text by S. Molian.
Also see the Schools Council Modular Courses in Technology *Mechanisms Pupil's Book*.

35 Patchwork patterns

This activity is a very good way into tessellations and plane patterns. It brings with it ideas of symmetry, area, angle, transformations, the concept of a unit of design and opportunities for geometric drawing and creativity.

It could easily provide a topic for a GCSE project.

36 Fun with subtraction

To quote from the teacher who sent me this idea, 'This has kept my children happily subtracting for hours. It's a nightmare to check when the numbers get big but I have a computer program to do this.'

So there's your next assignment ... write a program!

Because of the way the differences are formed the numbers will steadily become smaller and the end point will be reached in a finite number of steps. When the starting point has the smallest number opposite to the largest number the end point appears to arrive within five stages but if this is avoided longer sequences can be formed with surprisingly small numbers. Note that the smallest number can always be taken as 0 in any analysis for the differences formed from any given starting point such as $(8, 17, 3, 9)$ will be the same as that formed by reducing the starting numbers by their smallest number, $(5, 14, 0, 6)$. The solution below was found by a girl in a local middle school.

```
Start                  0   2   6   13
First differences        2   4   7   13
Second differences         2   3   6   11
Third differences            1   3   5   9
Fourth differences             2   2   4   8
Fifth differences                0   2   4   6
Sixth differences                  2   2   2   6
Seventh differences                  0   0   4   4
Eighth differences                     0   4   0   4
Ninth differences                        4   4   4   4
```

An algebraic analysis is difficult as it is $|x - y|$ and not $(x - y)$ which is being calculated at each stage.

It is interesting to compare this activity with a similar one starting with a triangle. How do the results differ? What happens with other polygons?

37 Gale

The main drawback with this game is the time it takes to draw out the playing area. If a Banda is available then several boards can be drawn on one sheet of paper in two colours and a large number of boards produced with minimum effort.

This game is discussed by Martin Gardner in *More Mathematical Puzzles and Diversions* where he gives details of an analogue computer to play it.

38 Guess the number

A useful space filler for the end of a lesson. It helps to develop logical thinking. Extending to 3-digit numbers is possible but may take too many guesses to find the number for most children who will then lose interest.

39 Trackwords

The hidden word is DISCOVERY.

The total number of possible 'words' is 784.

The problem here is to find a systematic way of counting all the words. A strategy and a notation are needed to ensure that no words are missed, and no word is counted twice.

1	2	3
6	5	4
7	8	9

The author numbered the squares as shown and then used spotty paper to draw out alternative routes before recording them as 9-digit numbers. By making use of mirror images and rotational symmetry it is clear that every fundamental route can be repeated eight times as illustrated here by the rotations and reflections of the solution 125349876. It is thus only necessary to find the 98 fundamental solutions. These can be subdivided into three basic categories.

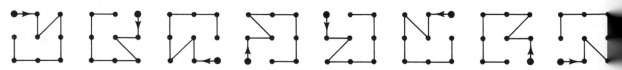

(1) A route starting at 1 and moving above the leading
diagonal the first time it leaves the leading diagonal.

There are 69 of these some of which are illustrated to
show their variety. They are given by the following 9-digit
numbers.

123456789	123486759	123495678	123495867	123498657
7689	7659	5687	5876	8675
9867	9567	5768	8567	8756
9876	9576	5786	8576	8765
123549867	123576849	124356789	124986753	125678943
49876	76894	7689	7653	768943
67849	94867	9867	125349867	126534987
67894	94876	9876	76	78943

126753489	126784359	126789435	126875349	152349867
3498	4953	453	75943	76
8943	5349	534	94357	152678943
9843	5943	543		

153249867	153426789	159432678
49876	98762	32687
67849	154326789	87623
67894	987623	

(2) A route starting at 2 and moving to the right the first time
it leaves the vertical line of symmetry. There are 25 of
these, some of which are illustrated here.

(3) A route starting at 5, the centre, moving towards 1 or 2
and then to the right. There are only 4 such solutions and
these are given by

512349876   512349867   512678943   523498761

This puzzle was originally suggested to the author by
Hugh Porteous from Sheffield Polytechnic, who also
supplied a computer program which generated the
solution.

40 Toasting efficiently

Let the three slices of bread be A, B, C with sides a_1, a_2, b_1, b_2, c_1, and c_2. Then the minimum time to toast the three slices on both sides is 107 seconds.

Time in seconds

Time	Action			
1–3	insert A		$\uparrow$	
4–6	insert B	a_1	$\uparrow$	
34–35	turn A	$\downarrow$	b_1	
37–39	remove B	$\uparrow$	$\downarrow$	
40–42	insert C	a_2		$\uparrow$
66–68	remove A	$\downarrow$		c_1
69–71	insert B		$\uparrow$	$\downarrow$
73–74	turn C		b_2	$\uparrow$
102–104	remove B		$\downarrow$	c_2
105–107	remove C			$\downarrow$

41 The prime gaps

An investigation into the distribution of the primes. Use a table of primes or a suitable program on a microcomputer. There are no primes between:

1129 and 1151, 1327 and 1361, 1637 and 1657,
1669 and 1693, 1951 and 1973.

It is easy to show that a sequence of non-primes can exist of any length. Suppose we want to show that a sequence of non-primes exists of length 100. Consider the sequence

$101! + 2$, $101! + 3$, $101! + 4$, ..., $101! + 100$, $101! + 101$. The number of the form $101! + n$ has a factor n for $n = 2, 3, 4$, ..., 101 so the given sequence of 100 consecutive numbers are all non-prime. This method can clearly be generalised.

42 Always one short

59 is the smallest number.
   The key to this activity is to realise that any number which is 1 less than a number which has 6, 5, 4, 3 and 2 as factors will have the required property. The smallest such number will thus be 1 less than the LCM of 6, 5, 4, 3 and 2. Further, any number of the form $(60n - 1)$ will have the same property.
   The same argument applies to the last part:

$$\text{LCM}\{10, 9, 8, 7, 6, 5, 4, 3, 2\} = 2520$$

so any number of the form $2520n - 1$ is a solution.

In particular the three less than $10\,000$ are $2519, 5039, 7559$.

When investigating this problem pupils often discover the redundancy of many of the given conditions, for example, if a number leaves a remainder of 9 when divided by 10 it will necessarily leave a remainder of 4 on division by 5.

The activity could be extended to cover (a) division by different sets of numbers, (b) leave remainders which differ by more than one from the number divided by.

43 Truncating primes

This is an interesting investigation to do. In building up the primes using the tree diagrams it is soon appreciated that even digits cannot occur other than as a 2 at the start. Similarly a 5 can only occur as the starting number. Also, when starting with a 2 digit it is soon realised that the following digits can only be 3s or 9s as a 1 or 7 will make the number divisible by 3.

The complete tree for the primes starting with 2 is shown below. There are 24 such primes.

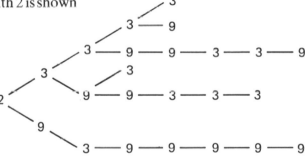

The remaining such primes are summarised by giving the number corresponding to the end of each branch:

31193, 31379, 317, 37337999, 373393, 37397, 3793, 3797.
53, 59393339, 593993, 599.
719333, 7331, 73331, 73939133, 7393931, 7393933, 739397, 739399, 797.

Anyone seeking further information should read the article by L.M. Chawla, J.E. Maxfield and Amin Muwafi entitled 'On the left-handed, right-handed and two-sided primes' in the *Journal of National Sciences and Mathematics*, Vol 7.

This activity has been about left-handed primes, but clearly an investigation could also be made into right-handed primes such as 12647 which remains prime when truncated from the left, or into two-sided primes such as 317 or 739397.

44 The tournament draw

At the end of the first round there need to be 16 (2^4) players left in to allow for a half of the players to be eliminated in each succeeding round. This means that 11 (27−16) players have to be eliminated in the first round. This in turn implies 11 first round matches involving 22 players, so only 5 players will receive byes. There will then be 16, 8, 4, 2 players in the succeeding rounds, i.e. 5 rounds altogether.

The number of matches will be half the number of players at each stage so will be

$$11 + 8 + 4 + 2 + 1 = 26.$$

But you could have arrived at this number much more easily. There is only one winner in the competition and 26 losers. Each match determines one loser so for a tournament with N competitors there will need to be precisely $N − 1$ matches to eliminate the $N − 1$ losers.

45 The police officer's beat

The police officer can patrol the beat by walking 2.6 km.

Consider the map as a topological network. All its nodes are even except B, C, I and O which are odd, so it is not traversible. However, a network with just 2 odd nodes is traversible (see activity 48 in *Mathematical Activities*) so by getting the police officer to walk between two of the odd nodes twice the remaining streets can be patrolled once only. B and C are the closest odd nodes so we get the police officer to repeat this stretch. The start and finish must be at O and I, the remaining odd nodes. One minimum route is given by

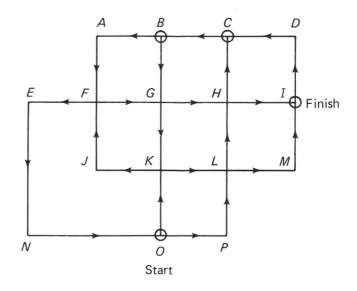

$O\,P\,L\,M\,I\,D\,\underline{C\,B}\,G\,H\,\underline{C\,B}\,A\,F\,E\,N\,O\,K\,J\,F\,G\,K\,L\,H\,I$

46 Coincident birthdays

Rather than considering the probability of birthdays coinciding it is easier to consider the probability that no birthdays coincide.

Consider first the probability that two people A and B do not have a birthday in common. Suppose for example A has a birthday on 25 March, then B's birthday could be any one of the 364 days remaining in the year. So the probability that A and B have different birthdays is 364/365. Now consider a third person C. For C to have a birthday different from both A and B gives C a choice of 363 days in the year, so the probability of C being different from B and C is 363/365.

Thus the probability for A, B and C all to have different birthdays is

$$\frac{364}{365} \times \frac{363}{365}$$

Continuing the argument for a fourth person D leads to the probability of

$$\frac{364}{365} \times \frac{363}{365} \times \frac{362}{365}$$

that their birthdays don't coincide.

Similarly the probability that in a class of 30 children there are no coincident birthdays is

$$\frac{364}{365} \times \frac{363}{365} \times \frac{362}{365} \times \ldots \times \frac{336}{365}$$

Patient use of a calculator shows this to have a value of about 0.294 so the probability that at least two children in a class of 30 have a birthday in common is

$$1 - 0.294 \simeq 0.7$$

It is interesting to note that the above argument shows that when a class reaches 23 there is a better than evens chance of two people having the same birthday.

47 The Embassy reception

Each ambassador shakes the hands of 79 other ambassadors. There are 80 ambassadors but each handshake involves two people which gives

$$(80 \times 79) \div 2 = 3160 \text{ handshakes.}$$

48 Narcissistic numbers

$$371 = 3^3 + 7^3 + 1^3$$
$$407 = 4^3 + 0^3 + 7^3$$

49 Getting to know the octahedron

Making the models described in this activity is very instructive. No amount of reading or looking at pictures can give the experience of handling the models.

The number of routes from one vertex of an octahedron to visit every edge once and return to the original vertex is 1488.

How many did you find?

It may help you to consider all the routes if you use a topological transformation of the edges of the octahedron such as that shown here.

For further reading see, for example,
Mathematical Snapshots by H. Steinhaus
The Third Dimension in Chemistry by A.F. Wells
Mathematical Models by H.M. Cundy and A.P. Rollet.

An alternative method for making an octahedron is to cut out a net of equilateral triangles, as shown, from paper or thin card. Score all the fold lines then plait the two strands of the net together starting with *A* on *B*. Remember that there are four triangles meeting at each vertex of the octahedron and this net should give you no problems. At the end, tuck the shaded triangle in and you will have a robust model which can be unmade and stored flat or made up to suit.

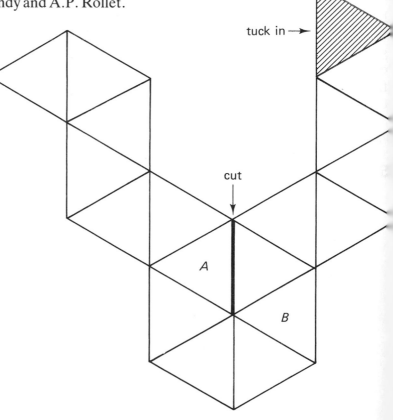

Net for plaited octahedron

50 The stamp machine

Mrs Royale Mail used stamps with values of 1p, 2p, 4p, 8p and 15p and this solution is based on that of designing the most efficient set of weights for a pair of scales. In that case weights of 1, 2, 4, 8 and 16 are used which allows accurate measurement of weights from 1 to 31. The extra constraint here was in the coins used which gave the total value of the stamps as 30p.

A solution where a stamp or connected strip of stamps can be found to give any value from 1p to 30p takes at least eleven stamps. The simplest solution is to take a 1p stamp followed by nine 3p stamps and end with a 2p stamp as shown.

This leads to an interesting investigation of what values to give a strip of n stamps to maximise the different totals which can be obtained from them (a) when stamps can be taken from the strip anywhere and used together (b) when stamps can only be removed singly or in connected blocks.

See also activity 51, 'Designing an efficient ruler'.

51 Investigating books of postage stamps

(a) The GPO's 1985 design is shown here. It contained three stamps at 13p, two stamps at 4p, and three stamps at 1p. This had the simplicity of design which made it very easy to find stamps for inland letters (13p and 17p) and also made it possible to find stamps to match all the other rates given except 38p, the rate for a 200 g first class letter.

Many solutions are possible, however, which allow all the given rates to be matched by a suitable selection of stamps from the book. Two are given below. The second of these has the distinct advantage that it could also be used for the time when the second class letter rate was reduced to 12p — in fact it allows four letters to be stamped at this rate.

This is a good investigation as it causes pupils to use arithmetic in a real situation.

(b) The impossible total is 18p. The 7p, 9p and 2p stamps total 18p but are not connected by their edges in the book. The other totals are made up as follows:

1p = 1	17p = 1+7+9
2p = 2	18p
3p = 3	19p = 7+9+3
4p = 1+3	20p = 7+9+3+1
5p = 3+2	21p = 9+10+2
6p = 1+3+2	22p = 3+9+10
7p = 7	23p = 1+3+9+10
8p = 1+7	24p = 3+9+10+2
9p = 9	25p = 1+3+2+9+10
10p = 10	26p = 7+9+10
11p = 7+1+3	27p = 1+7+9+10
12p = 3+9	28p = 7+9+10+2
13p = 9+3+1	29p = 1+7+9+10+2
14p = 9+3+2	30p = 1+3+7+9+10
15p = 1+3+2+9	31p = 3+2+7+9+10
16p = 7+9	32p = 1+3+2+7+9+10

This is a fascinating investigation to carry out and develops insight into basic number bonds as well as spatial awareness. Pupils have to make hypotheses and try them out. The question of what is the limiting value for N arises and one way of looking for a limit is to find how many ways a stamp or set of connected stamps can be removed from the 2×3 array. This last point makes a good starting point for a more general spatial investigation. How many ways can a stamp or connected set of stamps be removed from an $m \times n$ block of stamps?

There are 40 possible ways of removing stamps so this sets an upper limit to N, however the constraints of the problem limit the maximum value of N to 36. This can be achieved in the two ways shown below. Check in each case that 1p to 36p are all attainable.

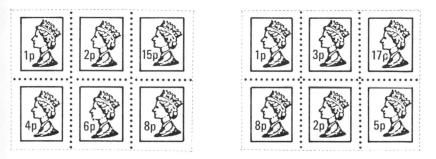

In investigating this problem it helps to consider totals both by building up (e.g. $12 = 4+6+2$), and seeing what can be left when stamps are removed (e.g. $24 = 36 - 8$ so $24 = 1+2+15+4+6$).

One way of approaching the problem is to start with a smaller page of stamps. With a 2×2 page there are 13 possible ways of removing a stamp or set of connected stamps and the two solutions shown here both allow 1p to 13p to be achieved.

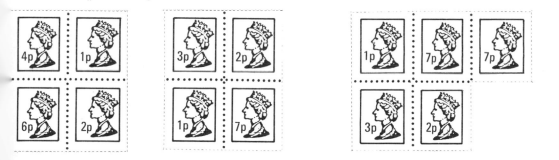

With five stamps there are 21 possible ways of removing stamps, but only 1p to 20p are attainable totals.

52 Designing an efficient ruler

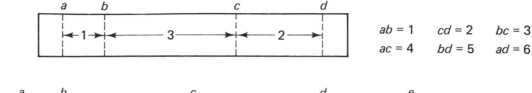

ab = 1	cd = 2	bc = 3
ac = 4	bd = 5	ad = 6

With five cuts the ten gaps are

$$
\begin{array}{llll}
ab & ac & ad & ae & \quad 4 \\
   & bc & bd & be & \quad 3 \\
   &   & cd & ce & \quad 2 \\
   &   &   & de & \quad \underline{1} \\
   &   &   &   & \quad 10
\end{array}
$$

and this way of counting them clearly shows the general pattern. With n cuts there will be

$$
1 + 2 + 3 + 4 + \ldots + (n-1) \text{ gaps}
$$
$$
= \frac{n(n-1)}{2} \text{ gaps}
$$

When the five cuts are spaced as shown above so that $ab = 1$ cm, $bc = 3$ cm $cd = 3$ cm and $de = 2$ cm, then $ac = 4$ cm, $ce = 5$ cm, $bd = 6$ cm, $ad = 7$ cm, $be = 8$ cm and $ae = 9$ cm. This is the best which can be achieved if there are to be no missing lengths. It is possible to get ten different-length gaps if we are not looking for a consecutive set of centimetre lengths. For example if $ab = 1$, $bc = 6$, $cd = 3$ and $de = 2$ then the following ten gaps are produced

$$1, 2, 3, \quad 5, 6, 7, \quad 9, 10, 11, 12.$$

When trying to produce gaps which correspond to a consecutive set of centimetre lengths then the best solution is to have the first pair of saw cuts 1 cm apart, the last pair of saw cuts 2 cm apart and all the others at 3 cm intervals.

With six cuts the lines will be at intervals of 1 cm, 3 cm, 3 cm, 3 cm and 2 cm and the set of measurements possible will be 1 cm up to 12 cm.

1 cm	3 cm intervals	2 cm

In general, with n cuts the set of measurements possible will be 1 cm to $(3n-6)$ cm. Why?

Compare this investigation with activity 50, 'The Stamp Machine'.

53 Number the sectors

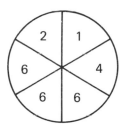

The diagram shows one way of obtaining the integers from 1 to 25, and represents the largest range possible.

Solutions for $n = 2, 3, 4$ and 5 are shown below.

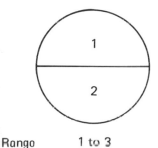 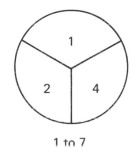 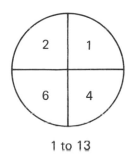 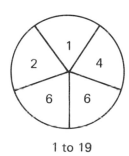

Range   1 to 3   1 to 7   1 to 13   1 to 19

It is very tempting to extrapolate from these solutions and assume that the optimum range is achieved by having the sectors numbered

$$1, 2, 6, 6, \ldots, 6, 4$$

when the number of sectors is four or more, but this is not the case. With six sectors the sequence

$$1, 8, 7, 4, 2, 3$$

gives the same range as the solution above, while with seven sectors

$$1, 8, 8, 7, 4, 2, 3 \text{ gives } 1 \text{ to } 33$$

as compared with only

$$1 \text{ to } 31 \text{ for } 1, 2, 6, 6, 6, 6, 4.$$

The difference with eight sectors is even more marked:

$$1, 8, 8, 8, 7, 4, 2, 3 \text{ gives } 1 \text{ to } 41$$
$$1, 2, 6, 6, 6, 6, 6, 4 \text{ gives } 1 \text{ to } 37$$

54 Three of a kind

Consider the first game. There are eight possible combinations of three numbers from 1 to 9 which total 15 and you may well have associated that total with the standard 3×3 magic square.

8	1	6
3	5	7
4	9	2

In fact the sets of numbers in the rows, columns and diagonals of that magic square give all the possible winning hands of cards as well as showing the relation between them and the game of noughts and crosses.

Each of the winning hands corresponds to a winning line in noughts and crosses so by using the strategy one employs in playing that game will give you a better chance of holding your own in the number game. Anyone playing first in noughts and crosses normally places their mark in the centre square because that position controls more lines than any other. Similarly in playing the number game the first player would normally choose 5 for it occurs in more winning hands than any other.

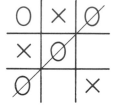

Using the link with magic squares enables you to adapt this game to other sets of numbers. Four such are given below, but see also activity 142 in *Mathematical Activities*. Try including negative numbers too!

10	2	9
6	7	8
5	12	4

total 21

9	2	7
4	6	8
5	10	3

total 18

13	6	8
4	9	14
10	12	5

total 27

6	⁻1	1
⁻3	2	7
3	5	⁻2

total 6

You should now be able to see what is happening in the second game.

Here the words have been carefully chosen so that they fit into a 3×3 array as shown in such a way that the words in a given row, or column or diagonal each have a common letter which occurs nowhere else. So again the winning sets of words correspond to the winning lines of noughts and crosses. MEAT is the key word and is in four winning hands while the corner words SARAH, BRED, EELS and BALL are the next most important as they each feature in three winning hands. The four remaining words are least significant as they only occur in two hands. With this perception of the game it can again be played like noughts and crosses.

This game in fact is a version of the game devised by the

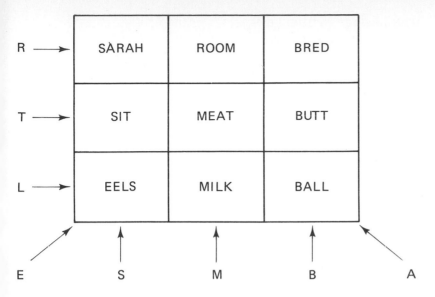

	R →	SARAH	ROOM	BRED
T →		SIT	MEAT	BUTT
L →		EELS	MILK	BALL

Canadian mathematician Lee Moser which he called HOT after one of the words he used.

It is quite an instructive investigation to give a set of more able children to devise their own set of nine words with the same properties.

But why be limited to words. Essentially we require eight recognisable symbols, one to correspond to each row and column and one for each diagonal. Then the nine cards can be designed by imagining them in position in the square, see the diagram below.

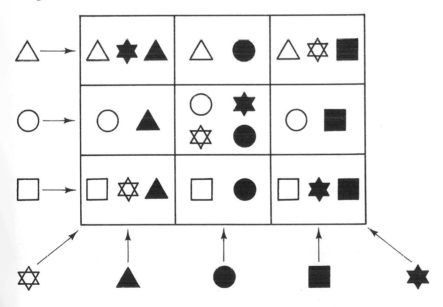

If you are artistic then the symbols could represent, say, members of a family, but whatever they are the game is essentially a version of noughts and crosses.

Now for the third game. Here the motorway numbers

165

should help particularly when you realise they go from 1 to 9, which matches the first game. Consider motorway 5, when coloured in it contacts the four towns A, B, C and D, and a closer look at the map shows there are exactly three motorways meeting at (or passing through) each town. Hence whoever controls motorway 5 has prevented their opponent from colouring three motorways at any of these four towns. This corresponds to putting a mark in the centre square of noughts and crosses which blocks four lines. Similarly motorways 2, 8, 4 and 6 correspond to the four corners as they connect three towns, while 1, 3, 7 and 9 which only connect two towns correspond to the mid-edge squares.

The duality between the noughts and crosses board and the Jam map is best considered by comparing the drawings below. The one on the left corresponds to noughts and crosses (each node corresponds to the centre of a square) and it is characterised by having 8 lines through 9 points with 3 points on each line. The drawing on the right is a topological equivalent of the Jam map and has 8 points lying on 9 lines with 3 lines through every point. The diagrams have been carefully labelled to show the precise correspondence. For example, points A, D and G on line s correspond to lines a, d and g through point S.

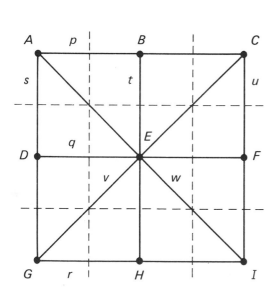

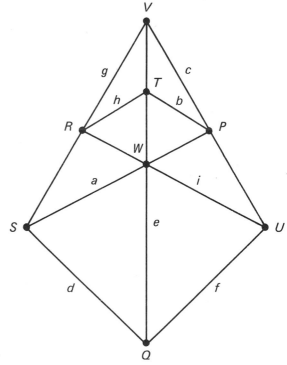

Getting through to the underlying structure and showing the similarities between apparently different situations is the essence of mathematics and these games when analysed give a very good insight into mathematical thinking.

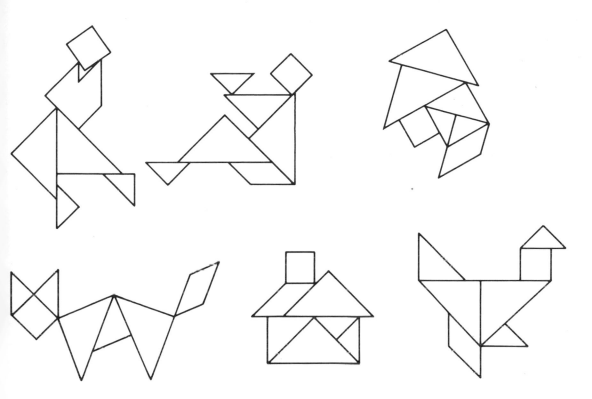

Tangrams can create hours of fun as well as giving valuable
spatial experiences. It is available commercially in a wooden
form as well as in a form for use on a magnetic board.

56   Rearranging the hospital ward

Two screens are sufficient as shown in the adjacent diagram.

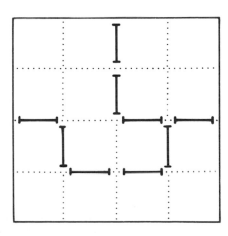

55 Make a century

$$3 + \frac{69258}{714} \qquad 81 + \frac{5643}{297} \qquad 81 + \frac{7524}{396} \qquad 82 + \frac{3546}{197}$$

$$91 + \frac{5742}{638} \qquad 91 + \frac{5823}{647} \qquad 91 + \frac{7524}{836} \qquad 94 + \frac{1578}{263}$$

$$96 + \frac{1428}{357} \qquad 96 + \frac{1752}{438} \qquad 96 + \frac{2148}{537}$$

58 Mixed doubles

The solution is not unique. One solution is as follows

	Court 1	Court 2
Match 1	Aa v Bb	Cc v Dd
Match 2	Ab v Cd	Dc v Ba
Match 3	Ad v Da	Bc v Cb

Note that there are six ways of picking two men from the four available namely AB, AC, AD, BC, BD, CD and similarly six ways of choosing the women ab, ac, ad, bc, bd, cd. The skill now comes in meshing these together to fulfil the given conditions. How many distinct solutions are there?

59 Ever more triangles and squares

This is an easy investigation to get off the ground but has much potential. The questions given indicate some of the possibilities.

Two equilateral triangles can be made by having one with an edge length of 3 short straws(ss) and one with an edge length of 1 short straw.

(*a*) Edge length 4 ss.

(*b*) One with edge length 2 ss and two with edge length 1 ss.

(*c*) Four with edge length 1 ss.

(*d*) or

(*e*) or or

(*f*) or an octahedron, but see (*l*)

(*g*) Edge length 3 ss.

(*h*) One edge length 2 ss and one edge length 1 ss.

(*i*) Each edge length 1 ss.

(*j*)

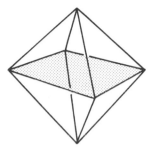

(*k*) a cube edge length 1 ss.

(*l*) An octahedron edge length 1 ss. Each face is an equilateral triangle, each plane of symmetry through four vertices gives a square, see the figure where one of the squares is shaded. Better, make it up by threading shirring elastic through your straws.

60 Pythagoras revisited

Most teachers of secondary mathematics have more than one proof/demonstration of Pythagoras' theorem at their finger tips but are not aware of the many fascinating methods and approaches that can be used. The collection of methods here is by no means exhaustive but they are the most likely to be meaningful in the context of current syllabuses.

The Pythagorean Proposition by Elisha Scott Loomis published in 1927 is a source of 250 proofs should you want to pursue this activity. It was republished by the National Council of Teachers of Mathematics in 1968.

61 The Maltese cross mechanism

The author has a model made up as described which has survived much handling and created much interest over many years. Within reason, the larger it is, the easier it is to make. In the author's model disc *D* is approximately 14 cm diameter and the mechanism is mounted on a piece of hardboard.

See also activity 34 for other mechanisms.

62 The geometry of rotary pumps

The study of mechanisms is much more meaningful to many children than the study of abstract motion geometry, but each throws light on the other.

63 Calendar capers

There are opportunities here for arithmetic, pattern recognition and the use of simple algebra.

When the total was 57 the dates are

$$\frac{57}{3} = 19 \qquad 19 - 7 = 12 \qquad 19 + 7 = 26$$

If the centre number in a column of five dates is D then the five dates are

$$D - 14, \quad D - 7, \quad D, \quad D + 7, \quad D + 14$$

so their total is $5D$. It is thus an easy matter to divide a given total by 5 and add and subtract 7s. When the total is 85 then $D = 17$ so the total corresponds to the last column on the page of the calendar.

If a column started with 6 then the fifth number would be $6+7+7+7 = 34$, but no month has 34 days.

If the first number in a column of four dates is F then the dates are

$$F, \quad F + 7, \quad F + 14, \quad F + 21$$

so their total is

$$T = 4F + 42.$$

Thus to find the dates from the total first subtract 42 and then divide by 4 to find F, before repeatedly adding on 7 to give the other numbers.

$$T \rightarrow \boxed{-42} \rightarrow \boxed{\div 4} \rightarrow F$$

The patterns of numbers for the cross and the H are

So their respective totals are $5C$ and $7C$ which makes it very easy to work out C given the total and then to deduce the other numbers.

The pattern for a 2×2 square is

D	$D+1$
$D+7$	$D+8$

So the products of the numbers on the diagonal are

$$D(D+8) = D^2 + 8D \text{ and } (D+7)(D+1) = D^2 + 8D + 7.$$

These clearly always differ by 7. This fact should be discovered by children given the right activity.

In a 3×3 square the sums of the sets of numbers given are all $3C$ where C is the centre number. The square cannot be magic however as the other rows and columns all have different sums, namely

$$3C - 21, \quad 3C - 3, \quad 3C + 3 \quad \text{and} \quad 3C + 21.$$

64 The travelling salesman problem

These problems are well worth discussion because they are highly relevant to real life. They are frustrating in that there is no known analytic solution but they are also easily understood and a challenge to optimise.

The shortest route for Mrs Lavender is 91 miles which is achieved as follows.

$$\text{Ex} \rightarrow \text{Oke} \rightarrow \text{Cred} \rightarrow \text{Tiv} \rightarrow \text{Cull} \rightarrow \text{Ex} \rightarrow \text{Exm} \rightarrow \text{Ex}$$
$$\quad 23 \quad\quad 16 \quad\quad 11 \quad\quad 8 \quad\quad 13 \quad\quad 10 \quad\quad 10$$

When Honiton is included the shortest route is achieved by taking the same route as before to Cullompton and then to Honiton followed by Exmouth and back to Exeter, giving a total distance of 100 miles.

As the shortest route never crosses itself it is in effect a simple closed curve so it would make no difference which town on it was taken as the base. However, if Mrs Lavender could finish at a different town to her starting point then she would clearly choose Okehampton to end the day, having travelled the route in reverse, thus saving herself 23 miles.

Finding the shortest route connecting the Dartmoor tors is an interesting problem as several possible routes suggest themselves. The author believes the route shown below to be the shortest but is willing to be proved wrong. (NB The changes in height, rivers to be crossed and difference in terrain which would be taken into account by the walkers has been ignored.) The length of this route is 16.6 miles.

In seeking shortest routes one needs to be aware of the increase in distance produced by diverting from the straight line joining two points A, B to pick up an intermediate point P. If $\angle APQ$ is not much less than $180°$ the increase in distance is negligible, but when $\angle APQ$ is acute there is a

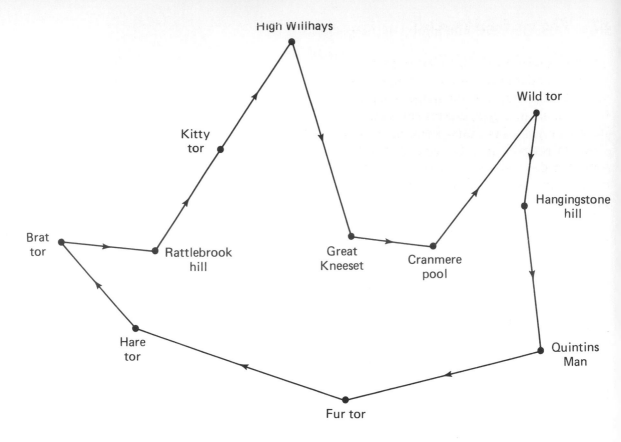

considerable increase. Consider, in the figure above, the diversion to pick up Hare tor when travelling from Fur tor to Brat tor and contrast it with the diversion to Wild tor when travelling from Cranmere Pool to Hangingstone hill.

For further reading find books on Mathematics and Management. Particularly helpful are:
Decision Mathematics by the Spode Group
Network Applications 3, Travelling Salesman, produced by the Sigma Project (a booklet with suitable examples for GCSE). For further information on these contact The School of Education, University of Exeter.

66 Transformation treasure trove

Dressing up combinations of transformations in this way makes them fun. Having solved one or more of these, children can be challenged to make up their own treasure map and clues on the same lines.

The treasure is at (7,3)

The route followed by the clues is

1 (1,3)	2 (4,3)	3 (4,7)	4 (6,7)
5 (8,5)	6 (5,8)	7 (11,7)	8 (7,3)

67 The variable menu

420 days pass before a meal is repeated.

The potato cycle is 4 long, the meat cycle 5 long, the vegetable cycle 7 long and the sweet cycle 3 long. Thus the first time the first meal can repeat is after $4 \times 5 \times 7 \times 3$ days, i.e. on the 421st day which is well into the second year.

As 100 is a multiple of 4 and 5 then rice and beef will be served on day 100. Further, as 100 leaves a remainder of 2 on division by 7, and a remainder of 1 on division by 3 the rest of the meal will consist of carrots and apple pie.

To find when roast potatoes, lamb, sprouts and apple pie are served we need to find the smallest number that

leaves a remainder of 3 on division by 4
leaves a remainder of 2 on division by 5
leaves a remainder of 6 on division by 7
leaves a remainder of 1 on division by 3.

The answer is 307.

Adding sausages and turnips to the meat and vegetable columns makes the four cycles of lengths 4, 6, 8 and 3 with an LCM of 24 so the meals repeat themselves every 24 days.

68 Loop-line limitations

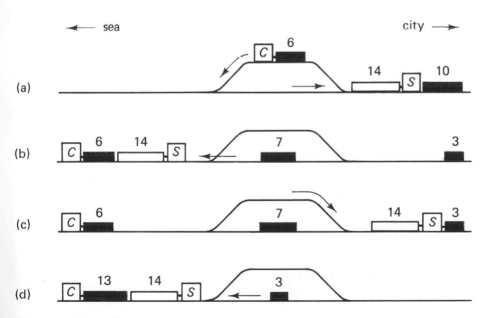

The train from the city, C, uncouples 10 carriages and takes 6 carriages onto the loop. The train arriving from the seaside, S, stays on the branch line and pulls up to the 10 carriages left by the city train. See (a). The train, C, on the loop now travels onto the branch line with its 6 carriages while train S pulls 7 of the seaside bound carriages along the branch line and leaves them between the points while continuing with its own 14 carriages until it is outside the points. See (b).

Train S now travels around the loop, and couples up with the remaining 3 seaside bound carriages. See (c). S reverses back along the branch line leaving the 3 seaside bound carriages between the points, and in the meantime C has reversed and picked up its 7 carriages. See (d). It is now a simple matter for train S to travel around the loop and to the city, leaving train C to reverse along the branch line to pick up its remaining 3 carriages before setting off for the seaside.

69 Which was the winning strategy?

Bruce and Christine tie for first place, followed by Daphne, and then Alan. To see why this is so imagine the race to be 16 km long.

Alan takes $1\frac{1}{2}$ hours, for 8 km at 16 km/h takes $\frac{1}{2}$ hour and 8 km at 8 km/h takes an hour.

Bruce takes $1\frac{1}{3}$ hours. Suppose his time is t hours then from the fact that half of this time is spent at 16 km/h and half at 8 km/h we have

$$(\tfrac{1}{2}t \times 16) + (\tfrac{1}{2}t \times 8) = 16$$

from which

$$12t = 16 \qquad \text{so} \qquad t = 1\tfrac{1}{3}$$

Christine running at a steady 12 km/h also takes $1\frac{1}{3}$ hours.

Daphne runs the same number of paces at both speeds but experience shows

(a) that the length of pace at the higher speed is longer than at the slower speed so she will run more than half the distance at the higher speed and thus take less time than Alan.

(b) the time taken for a pace at the higher speed will be less than the time taken for a pace at the lower speed so she will spend more than half of her time at the slower speed and consequently take longer than Bruce.

70 A topological trick

First Nuala takes her string at about its middle and passes it under the loop of string around Norman's right wrist, A, on the inside of the wrist and in the direction from elbow to hand. Next she loops the string up over his hand to the outside of his wrist. She should now be able to walk away leaving Norman and any onlookers amazed. Their own wrists will still be tied together but they will not be linked together. Be warned, however, if you don't follow the instructions precisely the strings can easily become more entwined.

For example, if Nuala's string goes from Q under Norman's string before looping around it to P, then Nuala will need to operate on Norman's left wrist as above instead of his right wrist. The only way to appreciate how this works is to do it with a friend, as many times and as slowly as it requires to follow what happens.

71 Parallel constraints

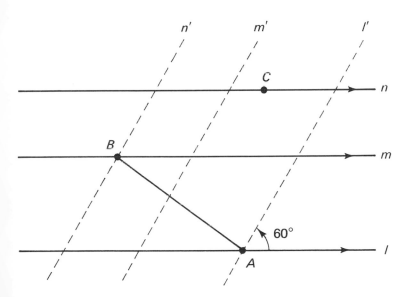

There is no need to get involved in trigonometry to calculate the size of the triangle.

Start by taking any point on l as A. Then use tracing paper and a protractor to rotate the three parallel lines l, m, n through $60°$ about A to give images l', m', n'.

Now this rotation will automatically map side AC of the triangle we are trying to construct onto side AB (look back at the figure on page 76). In other words C is mapped onto B so line n which goes through C will map onto a line through B. Thus B is the intersection of n' and m. Having found AB it is easy to complete the equilateral triangle ABC. Note by rotating clockwise through 60° about A we could locate C as the intersection of m' and n.

Constructing the square with vertices on the sides of a parallelogram can also be approached by using rotation. In this case because of the four-fold symmetry a 90° rotation is employed.

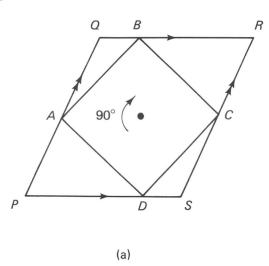

(a)

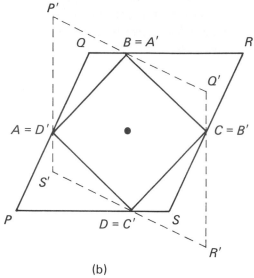

(b)

In figure (a) a square is shown in a parallelogram and in figure (b) is shown the image of $PQRS$ after a 90° rotation about its centre. The vertices of the square are clearly defined by the intersections as follows

$$A = PQ \cap S'P', \quad B = QR \cap P'Q',$$
$$C = RS \cap Q'R', \quad D = SP \cap R'S'.$$

The use of tracing paper to aid the drawing of $P'Q'R'S'$ makes the construction of $ABCD$ straightforward.

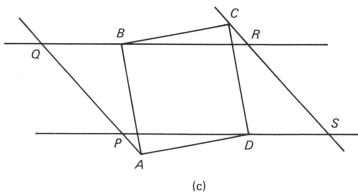

(c)

Figure (c) shows how two vertices of the square may fall outside the parallelogram and that the problem is really about finding a square with its vertices on two pairs of intersecting parallels.

See *Geometric Transformations* Vol 1 by I.M. Yaglom.

176

72 Hidden shapes

(*a*) This should not present too many problems. The halves
of *A* are isosceles trapeziums equivalent to the shape
obtained by cutting a regular hexagon in half by a
diagonal joining opposite vertices. The solutions are
shown below together with some further shapes.
Recording these shapes is best done on isometric paper.

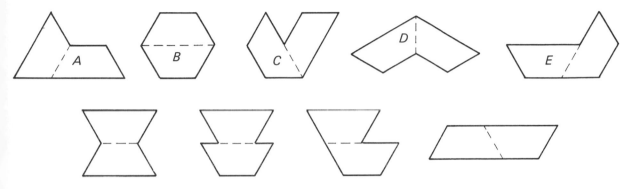

(*b*) The division of *A* into four shapes similar to *A* is shown in
(i). Other shapes which can be divided into four equal
similar shapes are easier to find than one first imagines.
Any parallelogram or triangle can be so divided and so,
for example, can the L shape and the half hexagon shown
in (ii).

(i)

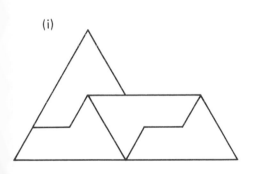

(ii)

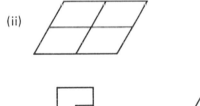

(*c*) Note the change in wording. Equal areas are required
this time, not equal shapes.

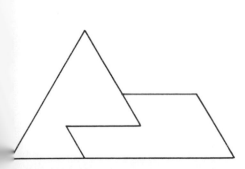

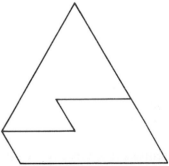

73 Sim

A simple game to set up and play, it is good for getting children to single out triangles in a complex figure apart from giving valuable experiences in ideas behind graph theory.

74 Boxes

This game is played by most children and can be used as a starting point for investigation work. It should not be difficult for children to find 'what if …?' questions and do some simple analysis.

75 Measuring the gear of a bicycle

Research shows that ratios and scale factors are one of the more difficult concepts for children to understand. Considering them in a practical context such as that envisaged by this activity should help the pupils' understanding apart from motivating them and giving them opportunities to apply their mathematics. This activity uses imperial units, since bicycle manufacturers have not yet changed to metric.

The gears available on the Claude Butler bikes are given by the following table:

		Number of teeth on free wheel				
		14	17	20	24	28
Number of	32	61.7	50.8	43.2	36	30.9
teeth on	40	77.1	63.5	54.0	45.0	38.6
chain wheel	50	96.4	79.4	67.5	56.3	48.2

Gear in inches with 27-inch driving wheel.

On the Ladydale cycle the gears, in order, are

30.9 36 43.2 48.2 50.8 56.3 61.7 67.5 79.4 96.4

and five changes of the chain between the chain wheels would be required as indicated by the arrows. With the Cresta 531 model seven changes would be required:

38.6 45 48.2 54 56.3 63.5 67.5 77.1 79.4 96.4

The gears available using the hub gears with the bicycle specified are shown in the adjoining table.

Hub type		Hub gear			
		1st	2nd	3rd	4th
	AW	49.8	66.4	88.6	—
	AM	57.5	66.4	76.7	—
	FW	44.3	52.5	66.4	84.1
	FM	44.3	56.9	66.4	74.8
	FC	49.8	59.8	66.4	72.5

Gear in inches with 26-inch wheel, 46-tooth chain wheel, 18-tooth free wheel.

Four sprockets which would give gear ratios approximating to the FW hub are those with 27, 23, 18 and 14 teeth respectively.

$$\frac{18}{27} \simeq 0.667 \qquad \frac{18}{23} \simeq 0.783 \qquad \frac{18}{18} = 1 \qquad \frac{18}{14} \simeq 1.286$$

A cycle with both types of gear would theoretically have 50 possible ratios obtainable but many of these would be so close as to make practically no difference. However the effect would be to extend the range considerably. Visit a cycle shop to obtain data on different bicycles.

76 Three-dimensional doodles

An activity of this kind was seen by the author many years ago in an art lesson but it could feature as well in a mathematics lesson. It stimulates 3D imagery, and helps towards giving children a way of representing 3D objects in two dimensions. Shapes made from wire coat hangers could be used as a concrete starting point although more able children will generate structures from their imagination.

77 Palindromic termini

There are many 2-digit numbers with the given property. Any number ab where $a + b \leqslant 9$ will always be a solution, for example

$$25 + 52 = 77, \qquad 32 + 23 = 55, \qquad 18 + 81 = 99$$

Further, any number cd where $c + d = 11$ leads to 121, for example

$$29 + 92 = 121, \qquad 47 + 74 = 121, \qquad 56 + 65 = 121.$$

78 About turn!

Trial and error will lead to many solutions, but to understand the problem fully an analytic approach is required. Consider the products set out as long multiplications

10^4	10^3	10^2	10	1
	a	b	c	
$\times$	d	e	f	
ad	bd	cd	0	0
ae	be	ce	0	
	af	bf	cf	
g	h	i	j	k

10^4	10^3	10^2	10	1
	c	b	a	
$\times$	f	e	d	
cf	bf	af	0	0
ce	be	ae	0	
	cd	bd	ad	
k	j	i	h	g

As the product is a 5-digit number $g \le 9$ and $k \le 9$. Further, no carrying can be involved at any stage, for it would occur in different directions in the sums and immediately upset the underlying patterns. This in fact is the essential condition and in terms of the digits it becomes

$$ad \le 9$$
$$ae + bd \le 9$$
$$af + be + cd \le 9$$
$$bf + ce \le 9$$
$$cf \le 9$$

This implies, for example, that if $a = 2$ then $d, e, f \le 4$, so for most solutions the digits will be small. However, large numbers are possible as the following example shows.

$$891 \times 101 = 89991$$
$$198 \times 101 = 19998.$$

Some further solutions are

$$123 \times 101 = 12423 \quad 123 \times 102 = 12546 \quad 100 \times 900 = 90000$$
$$321 \times 101 = 32421 \quad 321 \times 201 = 64521 \quad 001 \times 009 = 00009$$

79 Round and around

This makes for an interesting investigation at a variety of levels, for at the basic level it only requires the ability to divide by a single digit, but the patterns which arise lead to a variety of hypotheses which can be tested.

$$4\,|\,\underline{102\,564} \qquad 4\,|\,\underline{923\,076} \qquad 4\,|\,\underline{307\,692}$$
$$\quad\ 025\,641 \qquad\qquad 230\,769 \qquad\qquad 076\,923$$

$$4\,|\,\underline{820\,512} \qquad 4\,|\,\underline{512\,820} \qquad 4\,|\,\underline{205\,128}$$
$$\quad\ 205\,128 \qquad\qquad 128\,205 \qquad\qquad 051\,282$$

When dividing by 2 the same cycle of 18 digits occurs no matter what the starting digit is

$$2\overline{)526\,315\,789\,473\,684\,210}$$
$$263\,157\,894\,736\,842\,105$$

$$2\overline{)736\,842\,105\,263\,157\,894}$$
$$368\,421\,052\,631\,578\,947$$

$$2\overline{)947\,368\,421\,052\,631\,578}$$
$$473\,684\,210\,526\,315\,789$$

To obtain a similar pattern when dividing by 3 a number based on a cycle of 28 digits is found to be needed:

$$3\,103\,448\,275\,862\,068\,965\,517\,241\,379$$

The lengths of these cycles and the sequence of digits may stir memories of recurring decimals (see *Mathematical Activities*, activity 128), and a few trials with your calculator will show that the cycles associated with 2, 3 and 4 are in fact the same as those found when dividing by 19, by 29 and by 39 respectively. But how can we make the connection between them?

Consider $4\overline{)102\,564}$
$$025\,641$$

If instead of stopping after one cycle the process is continued and a decimal point is put after the 1, the division becomes

$$4\overline{)1.025\,641\,025\,641\,025\,641\,025\,64\ldots}$$
$$0.256\,410\,256\,410\,256\,410\,256\,41\ldots$$

Let

$$x = 0.0256\,410\,256\,41\ldots$$

then the division is of the form

$$4\overline{)1 + x}$$
$$10x$$

Hence

$$40x = 1 + x$$
$$\Rightarrow 39x = 1$$
$$\Rightarrow \quad x = \frac{1}{39}$$

Clearly a similar argument can be applied to all the divisions considered thus showing the link with recurring decimal cycles.

80 Insights into the icosahedron

Buckminster Fuller's works do not make for easy reading, but one of his books which contains much of his thinking on tensegrities is *Synergetics*. His models bring out very clearly which members in a structure are in compression and which are in tension and are reminiscent of some of the early aeroplanes.

81 Factors galore

Any such number must be a multiple of the LCM of 1, 2, ...
18, that is 12 252 240, and this gives a practical approach to finding all the solutions which are

$$2\,438\,195\,760 = 12\,252\,240 \times 199$$
$$3\,785\,942\,160 = 12\,252\,240 \times 309$$
$$4\,753\,869\,120 = 12\,252\,240 \times 388$$
$$4\,876\,391\,520 = 12\,252\,240 \times 398$$

82 Fascinating fractions

The solutions are not necessarily unique as the following show.

$$\frac{1}{2} = \frac{7\,293}{14\,586} = \frac{6\,729}{13\,458}$$

$$\frac{1}{3} = \frac{5\,823}{17\,469} = \frac{5\,832}{17\,496}$$

$$\frac{1}{4} = \frac{7\,956}{31\,824} = \frac{5\,796}{23\,184} = \frac{3\,942}{15\,768} = \frac{4\,392}{17\,568}$$

$$\frac{1}{5} = \frac{2\,697}{13\,485}$$

$$\frac{1}{6} = \frac{2\,943}{17\,658} = \frac{4\,653}{27\,918} = \frac{5\,697}{34\,182}$$

$$\frac{1}{7} = \frac{2\,394}{16\,758} = \frac{2\,637}{18\,459} = \frac{4\,527}{31\,689}$$

$$\frac{1}{8} = \frac{3\,187}{25\,496} = \frac{4\,589}{36\,712} = \frac{4\,591}{36\,728} = \frac{6\,789}{54\,312}$$

$$\frac{1}{9} = \frac{6\,381}{57\,429} = \frac{6\,471}{58\,239}$$

The author would be very interested to learn of any other solutions you find!

A similar problem is to find solutions to

$$\frac{ab\,cde}{fg\,hij} = 9$$

where $a, b, \ldots, j$ are $0, 1, \ldots, 9$ in some order.

There are six solutions

$$\frac{97\,524}{10\,836} = \frac{95\,823}{10\,647} = \frac{95\,742}{10\,638} = \frac{75\,249}{08\,361}$$

$$= \frac{58\,239}{06\,471} = \frac{57\,429}{06\,381}$$

83 How large a number can you make?

This is an interesting investigation in the use of notation and then in deciding which numbers are the largest.

2^{31} and 3^{21} are both large but which is the larger?

Now

$$\frac{2^{31}}{3^{21}} = 2^{10}\left(\frac{2}{3}\right)^{21} = 2^{10}\left(\frac{4}{9}\right)^{10}\frac{2}{3} = \left(\frac{8}{9}\right)^{10}\frac{2}{3} < 1$$

so

$$2^{31} < 3^{21}$$

When the factorial notation is used then the numbers can become enormous. Some of these are shown below in order of size.

$$321! < (2^{31})! < (3^{21})! < 3^{21!} < 2^{31!} < .1^{-(32!)}$$

The justification of this order is very interesting and shows how different the numbers are. For example

$$321! << 321^{321} < (3^6)^{321} = 3^{1926} << 3^{21!}$$

Similar very crude approximations can be made to justify the other inequalities and are left for the reader.

It is interesting to see just how large a number can be produced with the given constraints. The capacity of a calculator is left far behind.

84 Surakarta

The author had seen this game played in Java but forgot about it until seeing a description of it in *The Boardgame Book* by R.C. Bell. This is a beautifully illustrated book with descriptions of over eighty games from every part of the world.

85 Catch your shadow

B always moves in a direction which is +90° to that of *A* and through twice the distance. *A* will only coincide with its image if it moves to the point *C*, see the diagram where ∠*ACB* = 90° and *BC* = 2*AC*.

Try programming this activity on your micro.

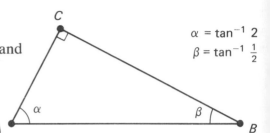

$\alpha = \tan^{-1} 2$

$\beta = \tan^{-1} \frac{1}{2}$

86 Number pyramids

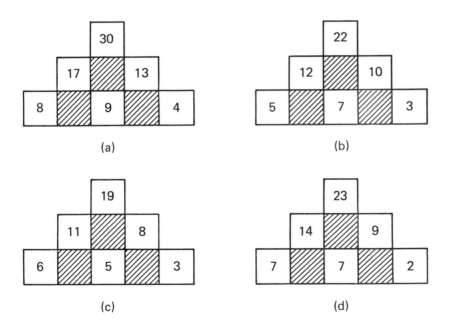

(a)   (b)

(c)   (d)

This activity has potential at many levels. Clearly the numbers could be made smaller, larger, include decimals and negatives to suit the individuals involved. It could also be used to introduce simple equations. Pascal's triangle is also lurking in the background. The pyramids can have as many levels as you like but not much is gained by going beyond say four levels.

87 Can you help the block manufacturer?

The dimensions of the block, to the nearest tenth of a centimetre, will need to be

$$15.9 \,\text{cm} \times 12.6 \,\text{cm} \times 10.0 \,\text{cm}.$$

To see this, suppose the block has dimensions

$$a \times b \times c \qquad \text{where } a > b > c$$

then, after cutting, what was the end face of the original block will correspond to the top face in the half block whose shortest edge will be $a/2$. Thus

$$a : b : c = b : c : a/2$$

$$\Rightarrow \frac{a}{b} = \frac{b}{c} = \frac{2c}{a}$$

from which $ac = b^2$ and $ab = 2c^2$.

Eliminating a between these two equations gives

$$b^3 = 2c^3$$

Hence

$$\frac{b}{c} = \sqrt[3]{2} = \frac{a}{b}$$

so

$$a : b : c = 2^{2/3} : 2^{1/3} : 1$$

From this it is interesting to observe that all the rectangular faces of the original block (and half blocks) are the same shape with edges in the ratio $2^{1/3}:1$ which is approximately 1.26:1.

As the half blocks have the same shape as the original they too can be halved to produce blocks with the same shape, and so on. This activity can be seen as a three-dimensional version of A paper sizes.

Why not make yourself a family of such blocks from polystyrene.

88 The Old Girls' reunion

Mrs Barbara Brown had duck.
Ms Bridget Baker had roast beef and an ice cream.

This is not such a problem to solve as it may first appear if tackled systematically using a table.

The full solution is shown below

	Miss Brenda Black	Mrs Barbara Brown	Mrs Beryl Burns	Miss Betty Broad	Ms Bridget Baker
drink	martini	sherry	martini	sherry	fruit juice
meat	steak	duck	r. beef	steak	r. beef
dessert	gateau	ice cream	gateau	fruit salad	ice cream

89 Amoeboid patterns

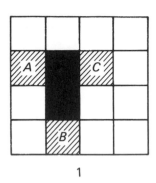

1

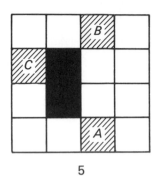

5

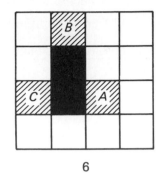

6

Each shape is made up of five squares, two of which do not move. The three other squares, *A*, *B* and *C*, however, slide around the two fixed squares in an anticlockwise direction, one square at a time. Shapes 5 and 6 are shown above. By considering each of *A*, *B* and *C* in turn it can be seen that they return to their original position after 10 moves, so shape 11 will be identical to shape 1.

The second amoeboid pattern has one fixed square while two of the other squares move together as a 2 × 1 rectangle. As before, the squares *A* and *B*, and rectangle *C* slide around the fixed square in an anticlockwise direction. However, whereas *A* or *B* would be able to circumnavigate the fixed square in 8 moves, if unimpeded, it takes the rectangle 10 moves.

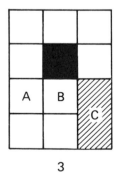

3

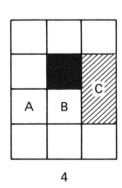

4

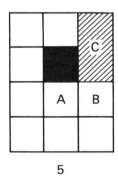

5

The result is that from time to time the squares *A* and *B* have to remain still while the rectangle *C* moves out of their path. This happens from shape 3 to shape 4 in the given sequence.

How many steps are required to get back to the original shape?

186

90 Make squares

This game is based on one by Boris Kordemsky a secondary school mathematics teacher in Moscow. See the translation of his book, *The Moscow Puzzles*, for other ideas.

The diagram above shows one way of achieving four squares.

The total number of ways of making up a 2 × 2 square is surprisingly large. Using shape E for example there are 8 possible solutions, see below.

91 Measuring the bounce of a ball

There is a lot of practical work here which can lead to straight-line graphs in a context where it is not difficult to motivate children. It also gives a good background to anyone continuing with physics or mechanics. The coefficient of restitution, e, has not been mentioned because it is not so accessible to children at the stage when I envisage this activity taking place. Also the standards for balls, when given, are in terms of heights. It provides plenty of scope for a GCSE project.

It is interesting to see the published standards for different balls.

Basketball	rebound 48" to 56" when dropped from 60"
Handball	rebound 62" to 65" when dropped from 100" at 68 °F
Lacrosse	rebound 45" to 49" when dropped from 72" onto a wood floor
Squash	rebound 28" to 31" when dropped from 100" onto a steel plate at 70 °F

Only the squash authorities recognise the importance of both the surface and the temperature in their standard.

A very good reference for anyone interested in pursuing this kind of activity is *The Physics of Ball Games* by C.B. Daish.

92 Seeing is believing

This result always comes as a surprise to the uninitiated and should evoke the response, 'Why does it happen?'. Put in the diagonal AC with another piece of elastic and you can then see that PQ is always parallel to AC and half its length. Similarly for SR.

The result is more general than may first appear. If AB, BC, CD and DA were four edges of a tetrahedron (i.e. not all in the same plane) it would still be true that $PQRS$ would be a parallelogram.

Try making a model from a wire coat hanger in this case.

93 Band constructions

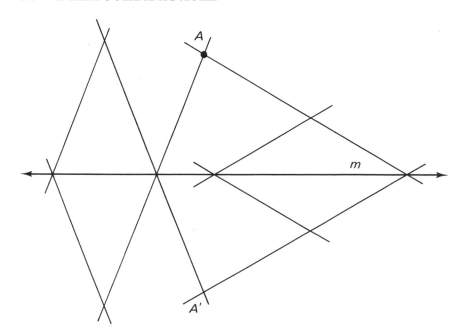

188

This is a nice activity to reinforce the properties of a rhombus.

The construction shown for finding the mirror image of A in line m is based on making m the diagonal of two rhombuses so that a symmetric pattern of lines is produced with m as the line of symmetry.

By joining A to A' this also gives a construction for finding the perpendicular from a point to a line.

For ruler and compass constructions see *Mathematical Activities*, activities 67 and 68.

94 Thwaites' conjecture

Trying to predict the length of the sequence from a given start number has so far been found impossible in general. For example, 27 takes 111 stages to reach 1, but who would have guessed? However, 2^n converges to 1 in n stages and is very predictable, e.g. $32 \rightarrow 16 \rightarrow 8 \rightarrow 4 \rightarrow 2 \rightarrow 1$.

This process is easy to program on a micro and facilitates the investigation. Further, it allows comparison with other similar processes such as computing $3N + 5$ or $5N - 13$ when N is odd.

There is a very interesting article by Bryan Thwaites on his conjecture in the *Journal of The Institute of Mathematics and its Applications*, Volume 21.

95 Cryptarithms and alphametic puzzles

Possible solutions to the first four mentioned are

```
        573
215│123195        25            96 233
    1075         ×25           +62 513
    1569         625           158 746
    1505
     645                  9567
     645                 +1085
                         10652
```

'FIT MEN JOG' was originally set as an addition sum in *More Mathematical Activities*, but as all nine digits are different it can just as easily be set as a subtraction.

It makes an interesting investigation to find as many solutions as possible. The following eight solutions have all been generated from each other. How?

$$\begin{array}{r} 790 \\ -132 \\ \hline 658 \end{array} \qquad \begin{array}{r} 790 \\ -658 \\ \hline 132 \end{array} \qquad \begin{array}{r} 907 \\ -321 \\ \hline 586 \end{array} \qquad \begin{array}{r} 907 \\ -586 \\ \hline 321 \end{array}$$

$$\begin{array}{r} 790 \\ -632 \\ \hline 158 \end{array} \qquad \begin{array}{r} 790 \\ -158 \\ \hline 632 \end{array} \qquad \begin{array}{r} 907 \\ -326 \\ \hline 581 \end{array} \qquad \begin{array}{r} 907 \\ -581 \\ \hline 326 \end{array}$$

And here are some further solutions from which others can be formed:

$$\begin{array}{r} 590 \\ -123 \\ \hline 467 \end{array} \quad \begin{array}{r} 709 \\ -586 \\ \hline 123 \end{array} \quad \begin{array}{r} 807 \\ -213 \\ \hline 594 \end{array} \quad \begin{array}{r} 783 \\ -659 \\ \hline 124 \end{array} \quad \begin{array}{r} 513 \\ -026 \\ \hline 487 \end{array}$$

With the slogan for MARS several solutions are possible. For example when $M = 0$, $A = 2$, $R = 5$, $S = 6$, $E = 7$ and $T = 9$, then B can be any one of 1, 3, 4 or 8.

CARL LEWIS has no solution but CRAM and COE have several outcomes.

$$\begin{array}{r} 7850 \\ + 72E \\ \hline 857E \end{array} \qquad \begin{array}{r} 5610 \\ + 54E \\ \hline 615E \end{array} \qquad \begin{array}{r} 8970 \\ + 81E \\ \hline 978E \end{array}$$

$$E = 1, 3, 4, 6, 9 \qquad E = 2, 3, 7, 8, 9 \qquad E = 2, 3, 4, 5, 6$$

but if $E = 1, 5, 7$ or 8 the solution is unique.

For further examples see:
Madachy's Mathematical Recreations by J.S. Madachy
Maths is Fun by Joseph Degrazia
The Complete Puzzler by Gyles Brandreth
Mathematical Recreations and Essays by W.W. Rouse Ball

96 Community coppers

This is an interesting investigation. Many questions arise such as:

Can corner coppers be avoided?

Will a minimum solution avoid two coppers looking at the same wall?

How many coppers are needed (*a*) on the perimeter (*b*) inside the city?

Ten police are required for the problem given and can be arranged as shown.

For a rectangular $m \times n$ city there will be $2(m+n)$ perimeter walls so $m + n$ police will be needed on the boundary. One must then find how many of these will be placed at a corner. An overall formula is not easy to determine but special cases can be found such as for $n \times 3$ blocks $2(n+1)$ police will be required.

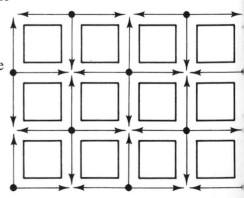

97 Exactly six primes

The solutions are of no significance but the activity leads to valuable thinking. Without resorting to operations four more solutions are possible:

2	3	5	47	61	89
2	3	5	41	67	89
2	3	5	7	89	461
2	3	5	7	89	641

Using such combinations as the following many more solutions can be found however:

$$3 + 4 = 7, 1 + 6 = 7, 1 + 4 = 5, 4 + 7 = 11, 6 + 7 = 13,$$
$$6^4 + 1 = 1297, 9 - 4 = 5, 18/6 = 3, 16/8 = 2, \sqrt{9} = 3,$$
$$\sqrt{4} = 2, 3! + 1 = 7, 4! - 1 = 23.$$

98 Magic polygons

Some solutions are shown below but there may well be others:

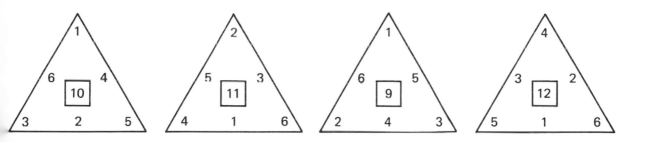

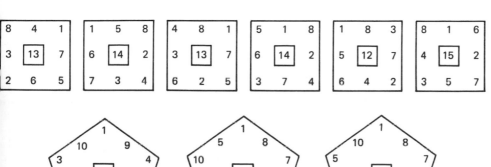

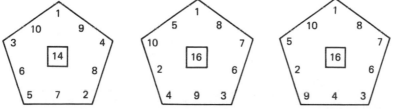

191

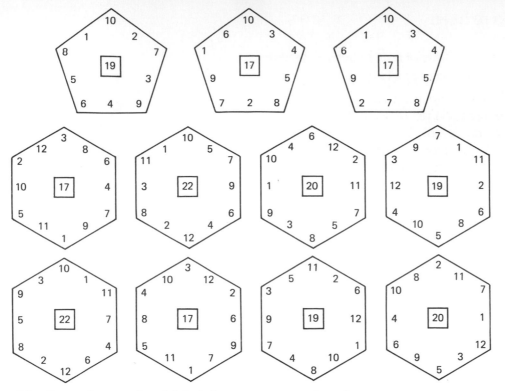

The first polygon of each kind above corresponds to the solution of that in the activity.

A close look at the solutions given will show that they are related in pairs. Take all the numbers in one of the square solutions away from 9 and it gives one of the othe square solutions. The number 9 is chosen as it is 1 more than the largest number used in the square solutions. Thus once you have a new solution the transformation $n \rightarrow 9 - n$ gives another.'

Similarly $n \rightarrow 11 - n$ and $n \rightarrow 12 - n$ will generate further solutions for the pentagon and hexagon respectively.

When trying to find a solution to a magic polygon it is helpful to decide first on a magic sum. But what numbers are possible for such a sum? Consider the hexagon which contains the numbers 1 to 12.

Six times the magic sum, S, must be the total of the numbers 1 to 12 (equal to 78) added to the total of the numbers at the vertices, as these each occur on two sides. The smallest corner total is $1+2+3+4+5+6 = 21$ and the largest is $7+8+9+10+11+12 = 57$ so it follows that

$$99 \leqslant 6S \leqslant 135$$

from which
$$S = 17, 18, 19, 20, 21 \text{ or } 22.$$

Suppose you decide to try 17 as a magic sum. The next thing to do is to look systematically at all the sets of three numbers from 1 to 12 which sum to 17:

12+4+1	12+3+2	11+5+1	11+4+2	10+6+1
10+5+2	10+4+3	9+7+1	9+6+2	9+5+3
8+7+2	8+6+3	8+5+4	7+6+4	

Then it is helpful to note how often each number occurs in a set. For example, 12 only occurs twice so it is advisable to put this into the hexagon first and then in the middle of a side where it will not be needed again. These strategies narrow down the field but trial and error and patience are still required. With experience further strategies recommend themselves but the above should give you a good start.

You may have noticed that some pairs of solutions have numbers in the same positions but two pairs of numbers have been interchanged. See if you can see what was necessary for this to maintain the magic property and give yourself another technique for finding new solutions.

99   Quartering a circle

Symmetric solutions, where the quarters are identical in shape as well as area, are not too difficult to come by, but unsymmetric solutions are not easy to produce accurately.

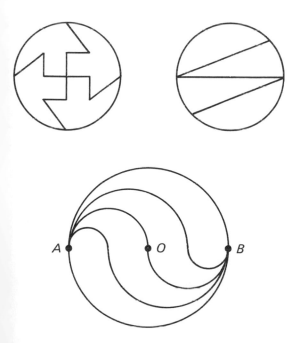

The solution using three curves of equal lengths based on emicircles of ¾, ½, and ¼ the diameter of the original circle s very satisfying.

100   Sweeping the park efficiently

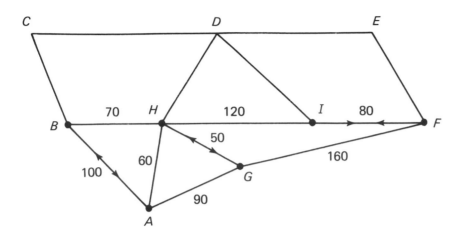

The network of paths has six odd nodes, A, B, H, I, F and G, so it is not traversable. To be able to trace out the network by travelling over each path once and returning to base each node would have to be even. (See *Mathematical Activities*, activity 48 for an explanation of this.)

The six odd nodes can effectively be turned into even nodes, however, if the route taken by the sweeper retraces three paths which join pairs of odd nodes. Three such paths can be chosen in many ways but the three which minimise the distance to be retraced are AB, HG and IF, which are marked on the map with two arrows.

Many routes are now possible which retrace these three paths to give a shortest distance of *1560 metres* (1330 m for the total length of pathway plus 230 m for the paths retraced. One such route is

   H B C D H I D E F I F G H G A B A H

The above explanation embodies a general strategy for finding the shortest route to traverse all the paths in a network. First locate the odd nodes then pair them off with the shortest paths available and retrace these paths.

   See also activity 45, The police officer's beat.

101 Connecting the fire hydrants

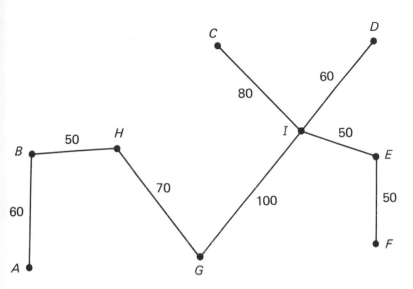

The best solution is that shown above, with total length is 520 metres.

The strategy for solving such problems is to start at any node of the network, say A then join A to the nearest node in this case B. Now look for the nearest node to A or B, in this case H which is 50 m from B and join it to B. Next find the nearest node to A, B and H which has not already been joined in. In this case it is G which is 70 m from H. Continuing in this way gives the above solution no matter where you start.

102 Traffic engineering

The maximum flow is 2000 cars per hour.

This can be obtained by 'chasing' cars along the network until the point is reached that any further increase would only be possible if the capacity of a road section was exceeded. However, this rather hit or miss approach can be made easier by employing the concept of a *cut*.

Consider the dotted lines drawn on the road map of the town. Any one of these cuts the town into two. Consider the

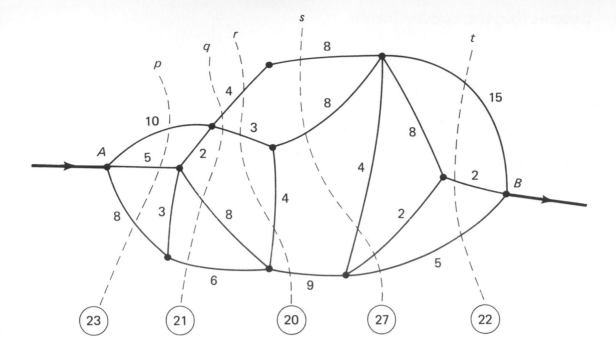

cut q which crosses four roads whose total traffic capacity is
$21(= 4 + 3 + 8 + 6)$ hundred cars per hour. This indicates the
maximum flow of traffic possible between the two parts of the
town on each side of q. Cut s similarly divides the town into
two but the roads which cross it can carry up to 27 hundred
cars per hour. By examining the network and putting in a
range of cuts, such as p, q, r, s and t, as shown, it is possible
quickly to get a feel of where the bottlenecks are and where
there may be surplus capacity. The *minimum cut* for this
network of roads is r with a capacity of 20 hundred vehicles
per hour and this immediately shows that the maximum flow
of cars across the town from A to B is also 20 hundred
vehicles per hour.

This answers the question of the maximum flow but not
how to distribute the traffic to achieve it. The solution to this
is not unique, but a solution can be built up by putting
numbers and arrows on the roads corresponding to the flow
used, noting that the roads which cross the minimum cut will
be at full capacity.

The solution shown here has been chosen carefully to
maximise the number of roads carrying no traffic. In this case
the four indicated by dashed lines. These could in theory be
pedestrianised or at least made out-of-bounds to through
traffic.

To increase the traffic flow through the town it is necessary
to increase the capacity of one of the roads which are crossed

196

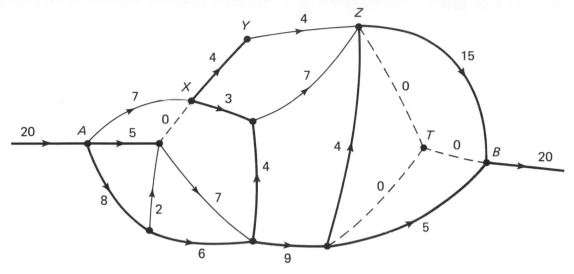

by the minimum cut. The best solution is probably to increase the capacity of XY (see above) from 4 hundred to 6 hundred cars an hour for this will change the values of cuts q and r to 23 and 22 respectively, making them equal in value to the cuts p and t. The maximum flow will then be 2200 cars per hour. However, the price of this increase is that traffic will have to flow along ZT and TB and so limit pedestrianisation possibilities. Time for a bypass!

103 The shunting yard

Uncouple the trucks between 11 and 12 and use the engine to shunt 10 and 11 onto b. Return the engine with 1 to 9 to c.

Uncouple the trucks between 7 and 8 and use the engine to shunt 7 onto b. Return the engine with 1 to 6 to c.

Uncouple the trucks between 3 and 4 and then use the engine to shunt trucks 1 to 3 to b and couple 3 to 7 and 7 to 10.
Shunt trucks 3, 7, 10 to a and return with 1 and 2 to c.

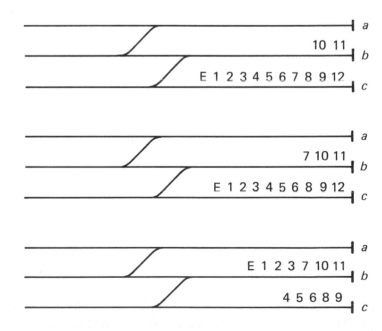

104 Sort these out

(*a*) $2 \times 7 \times 13 \times 97 = 17\,654$

The only plausible deduction is that the computer programmer was 26, her cat was 7 and her house number 97.

(*b*) $2 \times 7 \times 23 \times 59 = 18\,998$

The only plausible deduction from what we already know about the teacher is that the size of her class is 23, her telephone bill is £118, she had four sons and three daughters.

Pupils will find problems of this type interesting both to solve and to devise for themselves.

105 The ship's masts

It is impossible to find the distance between the masts. The height at which the wires cross will always be 2.4 m no matter what the distance between the masts.

From the diagram, using similar triangles or enlargement

$$\frac{h}{4} = \frac{a}{a+b} \tag{1}$$

$$\frac{h}{6} = \frac{b}{a+b} \tag{2}$$

Dividing (1) by (2) gives

$$\frac{a}{b} = \frac{3}{2}$$

Now from (1)

$$\frac{h}{4} = 1/(1 + \frac{b}{a}) = 1/(1 + \tfrac{2}{3}) \text{ using (3)}$$

$$\Rightarrow \frac{h}{4} = \frac{3}{5} \quad \Rightarrow h = 2.4$$

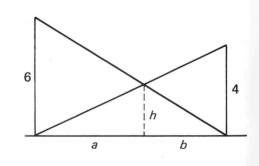

Another neat way of showing the independence of the height h from the distance between the masts is to consider a one-way stretch of the diagram from the 6 m mast.

106 Complete the set

The numbers are all of the form n^{10-n} where $n \in \{1, 2, ..., 9\}$ so the missing number is $343 = 7^3$.

107 1984 revisited

(a) $1985^2 - 1984^2 = 63^2$, an occurrence which last happened in 1860–61.

(b) $1984 = 2^{11} - 2^6 = 64(32-1)$ so one solution using eight '4' digits is
$$1984 = (4 \times 4 \times 4) \{(4 \times 4 \times \sqrt{4}) - 4/4\}.$$
$1984 = (2^8 - 8) \times 8$ so using $[\sqrt{8}]$ which gives the integer part of $\sqrt{8}$ we have $1984 = ([\sqrt{8}]^8 - 8) \times 8$ using just four '8' digits.

108 Kirkman's schoolgirls problem

day 1	day 2	day 3	day 4
195	296	397	498
278	381	412	523
346	457	568	671

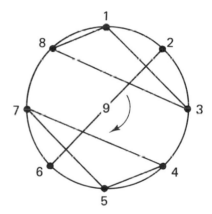

One solution to the 9 schoolboys problem is shown here together with a neat geometric representation of it.

9 is placed at the centre of a circle and the numbers $1, 2, ...,$ 8 are placed symmetrically around its circumference. A diameter and two triangles are drawn as shown which group the nine digits into three triplets. These correspond to day 2 of the solution given.

Now imagine the diameter and triangles rotating about the centre of the circle through 45° clockwise. They now group the nine digits into three completely different triplets. Repeated rotations of 45° generate four distinct sets of triplets which correspond to the solution given. Clearly by changing the order of the numbers on the circle many other solutions can easily be found.

The original Kirkman's schoolgirls problem is much harder to solve but a solution can be expressed using a circle and triangles as shown here, where repeated rotations of a seventh of a revolution are required to give the different form of the crocodile on consecutive days.

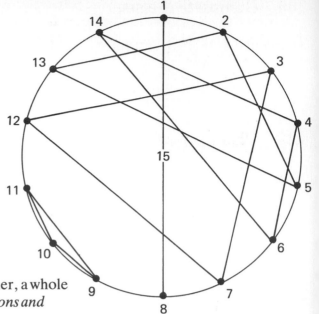

The position of the triangles shown corresponds to the crocodile

$$(1, 15, 8), \quad (2, 5, 13), \quad (3, 7, 12),$$
$$(4, 6, 14), \quad (9, 10, 11)$$

and following days can be found by leaving 15 untouched and adding 2 to all the other numbers where the addition is such that $14 + 2 = 2, 13 + 2 = 1$.

For anyone wishing to pursue this puzzle further, a whole chapter is devoted to it in *Mathematical Recreations and Essays* by W. W. Rouse Ball.

109 Food for thought!

(a) No, the answer is not 11. Only 3 socks are required.

(b) The first row is easy to complete, but then anyone trying an empirical approach will almost always try integers and not be able to complete the square. The point is that the magic total is always three times the number in the centre of the square. Using this fact leads to the number in the centre as being $6\frac{2}{3}$ and the rest follows.

11	3	6
$1\frac{2}{3}$	$6\frac{2}{3}$	$11\frac{2}{3}$
$7\frac{1}{3}$	$10\frac{1}{3}$	$2\frac{1}{3}$

(c) This 'proof' that $2 = 1$ can fool many people. The flaw lies in division by $(x - y)$ which is zero disguised. This and many other algebraic fallacies are discussed by Northrop in the chapter aptly called 'Thou shalt not divide by zero' of his book *Riddles in Mathematics*.

(d) $60°$, not $90°$ as often proposed.

Complete the triangle to see that its sides will all be diagonals of the cube's faces, so the triangle is equilateral.

(e) Interestingly P can be anywhere inside the triangle for the sum of the perpendiculars will be constant.

Consider a limiting case with P on AC. Then

$$PN + PL = x \cos 30° + y \cos 30°$$
$$= (x + y) \cos 30°$$
$$= d \cos 30°$$

where d is the length of the side of ABC.

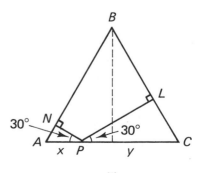

(i)

But this length is equal to the perpendicular distance from B to AC, see the dotted line in figure (i).

Now consider the general case, see (ii). Draw a line through P parallel to AC then $PN + PL = BT$ so $PN + PL + PM = BD$, the length of an altitude of $\triangle ABC$.

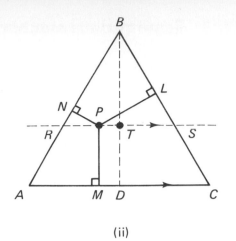

(ii)

110   Think again!

No amount of differencing or formulae will help solve this one. Each new line counts the digits in the previous line so

    3   1   2   2   1   1

is counted from the left as

    one 3, one 1, two 2s, and two 1s

and replacing the words by digits we have the sequence

    1   3   1   1   2   2   2   1

which is the last line given.
    The next line is then

    1   1   1   3   2   1   3   2   1   1

and the next

    3   1   1   3   1   2   1   1   1   3   1   2   2   1

With a little thought you can see that no digit can occur four times so 4 can never be in the sequence, or any higher digit for that matter.

111   Nine Men's Morris

Sometimes called 'The Mill' this game has been much written about. See especially *Mathematical Puzzles* by
G. Mott-Smith and *The Boardgame Book* by R.C. Bell.
    A modern game based on similar ideas is Kensington which was invented in 1979 by Brian Taylor and Peter Forbes, and is produced by Whale Toys Ltd, 55 Sidney Street, Cambridge. In this game the board is a network of interlocking hexagons, squares and triangles. The equivalent of a mill is to obtain three counters at the vertices of a triangle but then a player has the opportunity to move one of the opponent's counters to any vacant point on the network. This is a fascinating game to play and well worth obtaining.

112 Some curious number relations

Further examples are

$$63 = 6^2 + 3^3$$
$$175 = 1^1 + 7^2 + 5^3$$
$$598 = 5^1 + 9^2 + 8^3$$
$$1306 = 1^1 + 3^2 + 0^3 + 6^4$$
$$1676 = 1^1 + 6^2 + 7^3 + 6^4.$$

Another most unusual relationship is

$$4^4 + 3^3 + 8^8 + 5^5 + 7^7 + 9^9 + 0^0 + 8^8 + 8^8 = 438\,579\,088$$

113 Squared sums

D. St P. Barnard's puzzles are well worth collecting as many of them are of a mathematical nature. His other solution to a pair of 4-digit numbers was

$$(5288 + 1984)^2 = 52\,881\,984$$

This must be one of the few situations where addition is not commutative!

$$(0 + 1)^2 = 01 \qquad (8 + 1)^2 = 81$$
$$(20 + 25)^2 = 2025$$
$$(30 + 25)^2 = 3025$$
$$(98 + 01)^2 = 9801$$

The obvious question now arises, can we find solutions to

$$(abc + def)^2 = abc\,def$$

Over to you!

114 Matrix manoeuvres

This investigation brings together ideas on matrix algebra, geometric transformations and groups. At one level it is very sophisticated but treated as a search for matrices of order 24 in arithmetic modulo 5 it can be fun as well as instructive.

Two solutions are $\begin{pmatrix} 1 & 3 \\ 1 & 1 \end{pmatrix}$ and $\begin{pmatrix} 4 & 3 \\ 2 & 2 \end{pmatrix}$.

115 Odds on winning

Place £95 as follows:

£35 on Brigadoon so that at 2 to 1, should he win, you
would collect £105.

£30 on Tophatter so that at 5 to 2, should he win, you
would collect £105.

£15 each on Lightning and Virginsky so that at 6 to 1,
should either win, you would again collect £105 and
thus be certain of gaining £10.

It is a rare occasion in reality for the odds to be
balanced so that a punter could be certain of winning as
in this case. To see when it is possible find the sum of the
reciprocals of the odds plus 1. (Where the odds are of the
form m to n they must first be reduced to the form m/n to
1). When the total of the reciprocals is less than 1 you are
onto a winner.

With the race discussed:

odds of 2 to 1 correspond to $1/(2+1) = \frac{1}{3}$;
odds of 5 to 2 are equal to 2.5 to 1 which correspond
to $1/3.5 = \frac{2}{7}$
odds of 6 to 1 correspond to $\frac{1}{7}$

so the sum of the reciprocals is

$$\frac{1}{3}+\frac{2}{7}+\frac{1}{7}+\frac{1}{7} = \frac{7}{21}+\frac{6}{21}+\frac{3}{21}+\frac{3}{21} = \frac{19}{21} < 1$$

from which it can be deduced that for a stake of £19 it
would be possible to win back £2 by staking

£7 on Brigadoon, £6 on Tophatter, and £3 each on
Lightning and Virginsky.

116 Plans and elevations

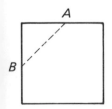

Possible side
elevation

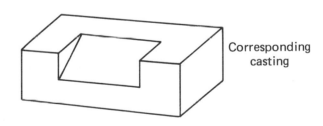

Corresponding
casting

One solution is shown above where AB is a straight line, but
it could be a curve.

There are many possibilities for three-dimensional objects, plans and elevations which can be started at a surprisingly young age.

How about a side elevation for the plan and front elevation shown here?

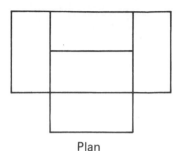

Plan

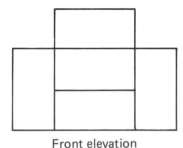

Front elevation

117   Thinking time

(a) The common error here is to think that the hour hand is still at 3.

The minute hand turns through 6° per minute. So in 12 minutes from 3 o'clock the minute hand will have turned through $12 \times 6° = 72°$. But 12 minutes is ⅕ of an hour so the hour hand will have turned through ⅕ of the angle from 3 to 4 (30°), which is 6°.

The angle between the hands is thus $18° + 6° = 24°$.

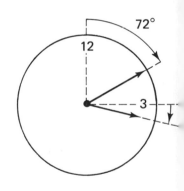

(b) Let the angle turned through by the hour hand since 7 o'clock be $\theta°$. Then the angle turned by the minute hand in the same time will be $210° + \theta°$.

Thus

$$\frac{\theta}{30} = \frac{210 + \theta}{360}$$

$$\Rightarrow 12\theta = 210 + \theta$$
$$\Rightarrow \quad \theta \simeq 19.091°$$

But 6° corresponds to 1 minute of time so 19.091° is equivalent to 3 minutes 11 seconds to the nearest second and hence the required time is

38 minutes and 11 seconds past 7 o'clock.

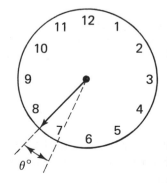

118   The Grand Prix circuit

The difference in distance travelled in going around circles of radii R and r is

$$2\pi R - 2\pi r = 2\pi(R-r)$$

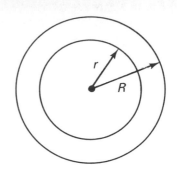

so for the car it would be 4π metres and it would be just the same for one lap of the circuit.

The actual radius of each bend does not matter and most of the right-hand bends are cancelled by left-hand bends, as will always be the case with a simple closed curve.

119   Robotics

One solution is r^2tr^3 which means first do operation r three times then operation t then operation r twice, i.e. work from right to left.

$$ABCD \overset{r}{\to} DABC \overset{r}{\to} CDAB \overset{r}{\to} BCDA \overset{t}{\to} CBDA \overset{r}{\to} ACBD \overset{r}{\to} DACB.$$

Alternative solutions also requiring six stages are r^3trt and $trtr^2t$.

It can be achieved with more than six stages but not fewer.

Anyone familiar with group theory will recognise t and r as generators of the symmetric group S_4. No knowledge of groups is required to do this problem and it could in fact be an introduction to the concept of a group structure. Anyone who wants to find out about groups cannot do better than read *The Fascination of Groups* by Frank Budden.

120   Improve your chances at Monopoly

There is a lot of interesting mathematics to be found in Monopoly and it is a game which most children know about. As a vehicle for introducing probability the author has found it works exceptionally well and beats into a cocked hat the more usual coin tossing ploys.

Most children seem quite unaware of the different probabilities of scoring the different totals using two dice and the approach through the context of Monopoly is received with great interest. It does help if you have a nodding acquaintance with the names of the sites on the Monopoly board ... but what teacher of mathematics hasn't!

121 The cyclo-cross race

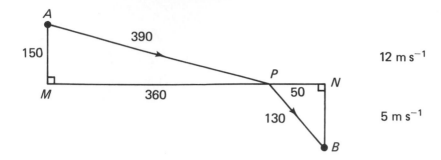

The diagram gives the optimum solution

$$t_{AB} = t_{AP} + t_{PB}$$

$$= \frac{390}{12} + \frac{130}{5} = 58.5 \text{ seconds.}$$

This is probably best attempted by trial and error using a calculator or micro to do the arithmetic. The theoretical solution requires the result that for the fastest route

$$\frac{\sin \angle MAP}{\sin \angle NBP} = \frac{\text{speed in first medium}}{\text{speed in second medium}}$$

Justifying this is well within the scope of an A-level maths course, using calculus, but then the equation to give the actual position of P is a quartic.

122 Carving up the camels

Perhaps deathbeds aren't the best place for mental arithmetic! The shares the elderly arab allocated to his sons do not add up to 1.

$$\frac{1}{2} + \frac{1}{3} + \frac{1}{8} = \frac{23}{24}$$

By the uncle's solution in fact they all gained.

Ahab receives $\frac{12}{23} > \frac{1}{2}$

Aziz receives $\frac{8}{23} > \frac{1}{3}$

Abdul receives $\frac{3}{23} > \frac{1}{8}$

This is a very old puzzle but well worth repeating.

123 The cranky calculator

The solution depends on the identity

$$(x + y)^2 = x^2 + 2xy + y^2.$$

From this

$$2xy = (x + y)^2 - x^2 - y^2 \qquad (1)$$

and xy could then be found by mental arithmetic.

However the calculator could be used to halve a given number X by using the identity

$$(X + \tfrac{1}{4})^2 = X^2 + \tfrac{1}{2}X + (\tfrac{1}{4})^2,$$

for from this

$$\tfrac{1}{2}X = (X + \tfrac{1}{4})^2 - X^2 - (\tfrac{1}{4})^2. \qquad (2)$$

Thus given two numbers x and y the identity (1) can be used to find $2xy$ and then identity (2) to deduce xy.

124 Calculator contortions

There are three main stages required to be able to find xy.

Stage 1
Square a given number by the following process:

$$\frac{1}{x} - \frac{1}{x+1} = \frac{1}{x^2 + x}$$

reciprocate to give

$$x^2 + x$$

take away x to give x^2.

Stage 2
Use this ability to square a number to form $2xy$ from

$$(x + y)^2 - x^2 + y^2 = 2xy.$$

Stage 3
Use the reciprocal function to extract xy:

$$\frac{1}{2xy} + \frac{1}{2xy} = \frac{1}{xy} \quad \text{reciprocate to give } xy.$$

You may well decide that if Betty Bolzano was clever enough to deduce the above she would have found long multiplication just as fast as all the key pressing this method requires!

NB Division could also be achieved as $x \times \tfrac{1}{y}$.

125   The chocolate manufacturer's dilemma

This is a packing problem. By using hexagonal packing instead of square packing the box can hold 50 chocolates instead of 48 and thus be of the correct weight. Instead of 8 rows with 6 chocolates there are 5 rows with 6 chocolates and 4 rows with 5 chocolates. To show that this is a possible solution use circular counters or coins. Theoretically it is not difficult to justify. In square packing the distance between the lines of the centres is $2R$, where R is the radius of the chocolates, whereas in hexagonal packing it is $\sqrt{3}R$, see the diagram. Thus the length of box required for the 9 rows in the hexagonal packing is

$$2R + 8\sqrt{3}R \simeq 15.9R$$

which is just less than the $16R$ required by 8 rows in square packing.

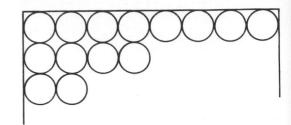

Square packing

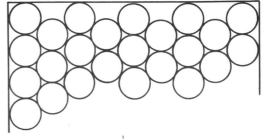

Hexagonal packing

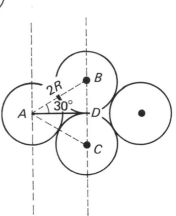

$\triangle ABC$ is equilateral with side $2R$

$AD = 2R \cos 30° = R\sqrt{3}$

126   The squash match

The scores were 9–5, 0–9, 10–9 and 9–5.

To do this puzzle you need to be familiar with the squash scoring system and also be aware that the only perfect number which could apply is 28.

127   Toilet tissue thickness

Don't be confused by the spiral winding. If the thickness of the tissue is d cm and the length of tissue on the roll is l cm then $l \times d$ is the area of the cross-section of paper on the roll.

Now

$$l = 240 \times 14 = 3360 \, \text{cm}$$

and the area of cross-section is the difference between the areas of circles of diameters 11 cm and 4 cm

3.5 cm

4 cm   11 cm

$$= \tfrac{\pi}{4}(11^2 - 4^2) \simeq 82.47 \, \text{cm}^2$$

so the thickness of the tissue $\simeq 82.47 \div 3360 \simeq 0.0245 \, \text{cm}$.

The thickness of all the turns of tissue on a full roll is 3.5 cm so the number of turns is $3.5 \div 0.0245 \simeq 143$.

This kind of analysis applies to most situations where some material such as sticky tape or rolls of cloth is wound on a cylindrical tube.

128   Stop the gaps

(a) 28   (b) 2310   (c) 24, 30

In the background to all these was the sequence of primes

$$2, 3, 5, 7, 11, 13, 17, \dots.$$

and the rules which give the nth term in the sequences are
(a) the sum of the first n primes,
(b) the product of the first n primes,
(c) the sum of the nth prime and the $(n+1)$th prime.

129   Multiplication squares

×	3	2	8	9
5	15	10	40	45
4	12	8	32	36
6	18	12	48	54
11	33	22	88	99

×	7	11	3	4
9	63	99	27	36
8	56	88	24	32
2	14	22	6	8
10	70	110	30	40

When making up multiplication rectangles of the second kind a minimum of $m + n - 1$ products will need to be given to make the solution of an $m \times n$ rectangle possible. For example with the 4×4 square it was necessary to give $4 + 4 - 1 = 7$ products to define the square uniquely.
   With a 7×5 rectangle, then, 11 products would need to be given.

130 Reinforcing the number line

It is the author's conviction that the problems found by school children and FE students with directed numbers stem from an inadequate image of the number line and that every opportunity should be used to help them towards a suitable image. When slide rules were used for multiplication many teachers used addition rules as a way in to them, but with the advent of the calculator they are now rarely used. This is a pity for their construction and use can give children new insights into number operations and the underlying structure of the number system.

See, for example, the *School Mathematics Project Book 1* chapters on decimal fractions and negative numbers for further ideas.

131 A fascinating family of square numbers

Consider any number in the sequence, say, 11 115 556

$$11\,115\,556 \times 9 = 100\,040\,004 = 10002^2$$

It is easier to see the underlying pattern, and how it will continue for all numbers in the sequence if we look at

$$
\begin{aligned}
11\,115\,556 \times (10 - 1) = &\quad 111\,155\,560 \\
- &\quad \underline{11\,115\,556} \\
&\quad 100\,040\,004
\end{aligned}
$$

Clearly numbers of the form 1000...4000...4 are square. Now we got this number from the original number in the sequence by multiplying that number by 9, itself a square number, so that too must be square.

The only other similar sequence is produced by expanding 49 by repeatedly introducing 48.

49	4489	444 889	44 448 889	etc.

In this case $444\,889 \times 9 = 4\,004\,001 = 2001^2$, for example, showing how closely related the two sets of numbers are.

132 Windscreen wiping

Suppose AB is of length L and PQ is of length $2d$ and that AB oscillates through an angle $\theta°$, then

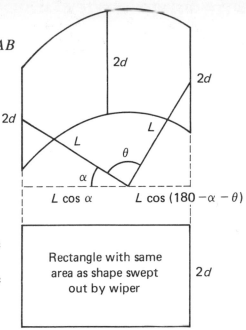

(a) For the car wiper the area swept out is $\theta/360$ of an annulus with radii $AQ = L+d$ and $AP = L-d$, so is given by

$$\frac{\theta}{360} = \pi(R+r)(R-r) = \frac{\theta\pi Ld}{90}.$$

(b) For the lorry wiper the area swept out is not part of an annulus as both the circular arcs of the boundary have radius L. However, as the vertical cross-section of the shape swept out is always equal to $2d$, the shape can be sheared into a rectangle whose dimensions are $2d \times l$ where l is the horizontal distance between the extreme positions of PQ.

If AB oscillates from α to $\alpha+\theta$ as in the diagram then

$$l = L[\cos \alpha + \cos(180-\alpha-\theta)]$$

so the area swept out will be

$$2dL[\cos \alpha + \cos(180-\alpha-\theta)]$$

Clearly this varies with α as well as θ unlike the car wiper which depends only on θ.

If $\alpha = 30°$ and $\theta = 90°$ then

(a) area swept by car wiper $= \pi Ld$
(b) area swept by lorry wiper $= 2Ld(\cos 30° + \cos 60°)$
$\simeq 2.73Ld < \pi Ld.$

There is a discussion of the advantages of the lorry mechanism in activity 51 of *Mathematical Activities*.

133 Intersecting circles

A torus has the required property.

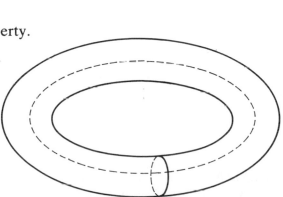

FURTHER RESOURCES

Books

C. van Amerongen, *How Things Work. The Universal Encyclopedia of Machines*, 2 volumes (Paladin)

W.S. Andrews, *Magic Squares and Cubes* (Dover)

W.W.R. Ball, *Mathematical Recreations and Essays* (Macmillan)

A.H. Beiler, *Recreations in the Theory of Numbers* (Dover)

R.C. Bell, *The Boardgame Book* (Cavendish House)

B. Bolt *Mathematical Activities* (Cambridge University Press)

More Mathematical Activities (Cambridge University Press)

B. Bolt & J. Hiscocks, *Machines, Mechanisms and Mathematics* (Chatto and Windus for the Schools Council Mathematics for the Majority Project)

E. de Bono, *The Five-Day Course in Thinking* (Pelican)

G. Brandreth, *The Complete Puzzler* (Panther Books)

M. Brooke, *Tricks, Games and Puzzles with Matches* (Dover)

R. Buckminster Fuller, *Synergetics* (Macmillan)

F. Budden, *The Fascination of Groups* (Cambridge University Press)

H.M. Cundy and A.P. Rollet, *Mathematical Models* (Oxford University Press)

C.B. Daish, *The Physics of Ball Games* (English Universities Press)

Dart Group, 5 resource books with ideas in a form to be used directly with pupils: *Shape in 2D; Moving in Space; Covering Surface and Filling Space; The Circle; Probability* (all obtainable from Devon Educational Television Service, Plymouth Polytechnic Hoe Centre.)

J. Degrazia, *Maths is Fun* (Allen and Unwin)

van Delft and Botermans, *Creative Puzzles of the World* (Cassell)

H.E. Dudeney, *Amusements in Mathematics* (Dover)
Puzzles and Curious Problems (Nelson)
The Canterbury Puzzles (Dover)

A. Dunn, *Mathematical Bafflers* (McGraw-Hill)

P. French, *Exploring Mathematics: Mathematical Puzzles* (McGraw-Hill)

J. Frohlichstein, *Mathematical Fun, Games and Puzzles* (Dover)

M. Gardner, *Mathematical Carnival* (Pelican)
  Mathematical Circus (Pelican)
  Further Mathematical Diversions (Pelican)
  More Mathematical Puzzles and Diversions (Pelican)
S.W. Golomb, *Polyominoes* (Allen and Unwin)
C.B. Grafton, *Geometric Patchwork Patterns* (Dover)
L.A. Graham, *Ingenious Mathematical Problems and
        Methods* (Dover)
D.J. Hancox, *Number Puzzles for all the Family* (Stanley
        Thornes)
G. Hawkins, *Stonehenge Decoded* (Fontana)
R. Hemmings *et al*. Network, a mathematics series for
        Leapfrogs, with titles such as: *Folds*; *Codes*; *Bands*;
        Pegboards; *Moves*; *Cubes* (Hutchinson)
D.A.Johnson, *Exploring Mathematics on your own: Curves*
        (John Murray)
B.A. Kordemsky, *The Moscow Puzzles* (Pelican)
R.F. Lausmann, *Fun with Figures* (McGraw-Hill)
K. Lewis, *Further Experiments in Mathematics: Geometry
        Without Instruments* (Longman)
H. Lindgren and G. Frederickson, *Recreational Problems in
        Geometric Dissections and How to Solve Them* (Dover)
E.S. Loomis, *The Pythagorean Proposition* (National
        Council of Teachers of Mathematics)
J.S. Madachy, *Madachy's Mathematical Recreations*
        (Dover)
R. McKim, *101 Patchwork Patterns* (Dover)
S. Molian, *Mechanism Design, an Introductory Text*
        (Cambridge University Press)
L. Mottershead, *Sources of Mathematical Discovery* (Basil
        Blackwell)
G. Mott-Smith, *Mathematical Puzzles* (Dover)
H.J.R. Murray, *A History of Board Games* (Oxford
        University Press)
E.P. Northrop, *Riddles in Mathematics* (Pelican)
Schools Council Modular Courses in Technology,
        Mechanisms (Oliver and Boyd in association with the
        National Council for School Technology)
Spode Group, *Decision Mathematics* (Ellis Horwood)
H. Steinhaus, *Mathematical Snapshots* (Oxford University
        Press)
S. Strondh, *Machines, an Illustrated History* (Nordbok)
A.F. Wells, *The Third Dimension in Chemistry* (Oxford
        University Press)
J.E. Wood, *Sun, Moon and Standing Stones* (Oxford
        University Press)
I.M. Yaglom, translated by A. Shields from the Russian,
        Geometric Transformations Vol. 1 (Random House)

Magazines

Factor, produced for children by teachers through the SMILE Centre, Middle Row School, Kensal Road, London W10

Mathematical Pie, published for secondary children, available from West View, Fiveways, Nr. Warwick

Number, a magazine for lower secondary school children published termly by Resources for Learning Development Unit, Bishop Road, Bishopston, Bristol BS7 8LS

Mathematics in School, a source of many good ideas for secondary teachers, published 5 times a year on behalf of The Mathematical Association by Longman Group, Westgate House, The High, Harlow, CM20 1NE

Mathematics Teaching, for school teachers at all levels, and published by the Association of Teachers of Mathematics, King's Chamber, Queen Street, Derby, DE1 3DA

Teaching Mathematics and its Applications, for secondary teachers, is published by the Institute of Mathematics and its Applications, Maitland House, Warrior Square, Southend-on-Sea, Essex, SS1 2JY

The Mathematical Gazette, mainly for sixth form teachers, published by The Mathematical Association, 259 London Road, Leicester LE2 3BE

The Arithmetic Teacher, and *The Mathematics Teacher*, both published by the National Council of Teachers of Mathematics, 1906 Association Drive, Reston, Virginia 22091, USA

Other sources

Double Games Ltd, 10 Hampstead Gardens, London NW

Games Centre, 16 Hamway Street, London W1A 2LS

Pentangle, Over Wallop, Hants SO20 8NT

Pictorial Charts Educational Trust, 27 Kirchen Road, London W13 0UD

Tarquin Publications (a treasure house of games, books and posters), Stradbroke, Diss, Norfolk IP21 5JP

INDEX

NB The numbers refer to the
activity not the page.